Knitting Fabric Rugs

Knitting FABRIC RUGS

28 Colorful Designs
for Crafters of Every Level

KAREN TIEDE

Photography by Kip Dawkins

 Storey Publishing

*The mission of Storey Publishing is to serve our customers by
publishing practical information that encourages
personal independence in harmony with the environment.*

Edited by Gwen Steege
Art direction and book design by Alethea Morrison
Text production by Jennifer Jepson Smith

Cover photography by © Kip Dawkins Photography, except for Charles Gupton (author) and
    Mars Vilaubi (inside front cover)
Interior photography by © Kip Dawkins Photography, except for: © Kimberley Coole/Getty
    Images, 29; Mars Vilaubi, 33, 61, 75, 93, 101 (bottom), 116, 123, 128 (bottom), 135, 146 (top),
    167; © raciro/iStockphoto.com, 55 (left)
Photo styling by Neely Dykshorn
Illustrations by Alethea Morrison, except: Moses Harris, courtesy of Wikimedia Commons 11
Charts by Ilona Sherratt
Indexed by Nancy D. Wood

Storey Publishing
210 MASS MoCA Way
North Adams, MA 01247
www.storey.com

Printed in China by Toppan Leefung Printing Ltd.
10 9 8 7 6 5 4 3 2 1

LIBRARY OF CONGRESS CATALOGING-IN-PUBLICATION DATA

Tiede, Karen.
 Knitted fabric rugs : 28 colorful designs for crafters of every level / Karen Tiede.
    pages cm
 ISBN 978-1-61212-448-3 (pbk. : alk. paper)
 ISBN 978-1-61212-449-0 (ebook) 1. Rugs. 2. Knitting—Patterns. I. Title.
 TT850.T53 2015
 746.7'3—dc23
                                                    2015008211

To my mother,
who taught me
to knit

Contents

Knitted Rugs
The Backstory

I have been a knitter all my conscious life. I can't remember not knowing how to knit. I recall a bulky sweater jacket I knit as a freshman in high school, and knee socks with clock designs knit sometime before graduation. There was an afghan in there, also — at least one or two. My mother knits (my father never wore store-bought winter socks), her mother knit, and her mother before that.

I discovered Kaffe Fassett in 1986 during grad school in western Massachusetts. A friend bought me his first popular book, *Glorious Color*, and I knitted her a sweater in return. Next there was a Fassett vest and an argyle sweater. I discovered the grab bags at WEBS yarn store in Northampton, Massachusetts, and I knit on the cheap. I knitted sweaters for everyone in my family, and none of them fit: something for Eric in green Lopi, which knit very quickly; something with cables for Paul. Eventually, I learned not to knit sweaters for men I wasn't married to.

Then I moved to North Carolina, where it's warm most of the time, and the sweater season is less than four months long. Still, I continued to knit. Tried cotton and didn't like the way it hung. Tried Fair Isle in the wrong colors for me. I knit a completely complicated Aran in the round, followed by Fassett's Tumbling Blocks sweater, and entered it in the state fair. The judge said the buttons were gaudy, and I never entered the state fair again. It wasn't just the buttons: the gauge was all wrong, and the sweater never fit. It took two more Fassett intarsia sweaters to teach me, the hard way, that a swatch knit without intarsia doesn't give the gauge you get when you knit the whole garment in an intarsia pattern.

I continued to knit, but because I lived in a warm state, I turned to projects other than garments. I made a knitted lace tablecloth for my brother and his wife as a wedding present (6 *miles* of thread) and finished it before the birth of their first child. When I went on a 28-day tour of Antarctica for the Y2K turn-of-the-millennium, I knitted socks on the way and bought lots of New Zealand wool. When I came back, however, I was so overwhelmed by Antarctica that I couldn't bear to knit, and hung up my circulars for what turned out to be four years.

Became a chainsaw carver and even edited a book titled *Carve Smart: 100 Chainsaw Carvers from around the World Answer Questions about Chainsaw Carving.* I sold my chainsaw art, but I also discovered how heavy chainsaw art is, how hard it is to sell, and how ephemeral wood art is in a state that has termites.

Then one day, four years after hanging up the needles, I thought about knitting again. There was a reason I hadn't recycled my yarn stash, despite all the Feng Shui advice to the contrary. My best friend gave me *The Knitting Sutra* for Christmas. I read the book straight through over breakfast, cast on before lunch, and had the ribbing for the back of a sweater done by dinnertime.

Why Knitted Rugs?

My extended family goes to the Outer Banks every summer. While we were in Manteo, North Carolina, on a gray and blustery beach afternoon, we stopped at the Endless Possibilities gallery mentioned in

Niche magazine. Their promo said "Endless Possibilities is an innovative recycling project that utilizes castoff clothing items from Hotline's fundraising thrift shops to weave new fabric that is transformed into rugs, totes, and other useful and attractive items."

Having been a volunteer on a thrift-shop sorting crew in the past, I could identify the component clothing in the weavings in Endless Possibilities' gallery. The weavers cut strips of clothing and used them as weft, selecting colors to coordinate. At the time, I had no interest in weaving but could see that the raw material could be knit or crocheted.

I needed a new bathroom rug, had access to T-shirts, and found a pattern for knitting a bathroom rug out of T-shirts in Leigh Radford's *Alterknits*. That was the beginning. I knit one rug, then another. My art form was born. It met all criteria: climate independent, cheap, fast, colorful, challenging. I already had all the art-business information needed from my stint as a chainsaw carver and knew that I could figure out how to sell rugs. And there was no end to the raw material.

The 100-Rug Challenge

Somewhere very early in the process, I decided to make 100 rugs, based on a suggestion found in David Bayles and Ted Orland's *Art & Fear: Observations on the Peril (and Rewards) of Artmaking,* the best book about creativity that I have ever read. The

book contends that the best artists make the most art. Committing to a series of 100 rugs eliminated any fear of failure. I wasn't trying to make one good rug or the ultimate rug or a perfect rug; I was going to make 100 rugs and see what happened. Every time I made a rug, the rug itself would provide ideas for what could happen in the next rug. This concept is actually true for all creative endeavors. The most perfect idea becomes more interesting as it is committed to form. Test, and more options appear. The possibilities multiply.

The first rug was straight stripes knitted in four panels. For the second, I knitted six blocks, doing a pickup as I turned the corner and started back with the second color. (It took me at least twelve rugs to understand the garter-stitch color-change problem; see page 40.) The color selection became more interesting as I grew my stash. (We'll talk about stash in chapter 1.) I discovered methods of knitting that I liked and methods that I didn't. I'm old enough and cantankerous enough, and have read enough Elizabeth Zimmermann, to be ruthless about tossing stuff off the boat if I don't like doing it. This is supposed to be fun. If it's not feeling good, why do it? Some of my constraints are age-related and physical. My hands hurt. If I were going to do 100 rugs, I couldn't afford to do anything that made my hands hurt more than they already did.

Constraints That Offer Possibility

The biggest constraint I faced when deciding to knit rugs was ergonomic. I solved it by making the decision to work in garter stitch rather than in stockinette, which requires alternating rows of knit and purl. Purling at 2 stitches to the inch hurts the extensor muscles (the ones that straighten your fingers) in my dominant hand. I can't afford to lose hand dexterity, so garter stitch is a better option, because I can knit every row. Garter stitch offers more advantages than just ergonomics, however, including the fact that its structure results in a springy fabric that stretches fairly evenly in both directions. (For more about the characteristics of garter stitch, see page 39.)

Another ergonomic consideration made me decide to limit the number of stitches on the needle to 12. I can go to 22 stitches in a pinch, but it starts to hurt. So the designs are planned as small units. Knitting is generally a stripy sort of art form. However, when the knitted units are a fixed width, you can move them around in the design to create color areas that are larger than the width of the stripes. You can also turn units so that the stripes move in different directions.

The design possibilities are endless, and those possibilities have led me to push the envelope when exploring what can be done with stripes, as well as quilt patterns like tessellations and log cabin, then move on to spirals and triple spirals, and finally to freeform designs. In the pages that follow, I offer patterns for each of these techniques, as well as explanations of the thinking that's behind many of these designs.

But the Music Is Better in My Head!

All design starts with constraints. The universe of what is theoretically possible is infinite; the subset of what you can actually create with fiber is limited. Constraints are what bring the two sets together. The perfect work of art exists only in my imagination. The second I start making decisions about an actual, versus a theoretical, work of art, limitations and constraints enter the picture, along with compromises and dead ends (meaning, knitting that needs to be unpicked).

After many years of making and selling art and hanging out with people who make and sell art, I now know that real artists understand the limits and process. Not that we have a vision particularly, or that we see the world any differently. To me, an artist is a person who:

- Lives with constraints and moves forward anyway

- Can manage, at least for the time it takes to make something, the chatter of voices in his head

- Provides the time, opportunity, and physical structure to let ideas develop

- Gives herself permission to have inventory (to knitters, this is stash), so that ideas that need to be tested can be acted upon, in real time, not held in abeyance for a trip to the store

Isn't Everyone Creative?

It's very painful to hear people say, "I'm not creative." Of course you're creative! But muses are delicate; if you tell them you don't want their company, they'll believe you. Working artists know that the muses are always around us, but they tend to speak more when we're already working, passing us an unexpected color, a sideways look at something, a whisper of, "Why not turn it upside down?" Muses simply don't give good ideas to people who announce that they're not willing to play. However, I'm able to give life to perhaps only one out of 50 ideas that cross my mind. Sometimes people suggest I try to focus and not do quite so many different kinds of art. This is an unfathomable concept. It would be easier to become short and blonde than to "focus on one thing."

Ideas are cheap, easy, and abundant. The world can be divided into two groups of people: those who think ideas are valuable in and of themselves, and those who know the real value is in the development or execution, not the idea itself. I'm in the latter camp. Am I someone who knits rugs, or someone who merely collects old clothes and talks about the rugs I could knit? Someone who makes art, or someone who talks about all the art she could make

if she didn't have to work, shop, do the rest of her life?

I also believe that ideas have lives of their own. At last count, I had 52 notebooks filled with ideas that I had written down or somehow illustrated and documented. I have no good understanding of how to determine which ideas are going to take form; it simply happens. In general, I let ideas ripen in the notebooks rather than talk about them. At some point, a few ideas become a finished product.

I don't know that I have ever had a completely original idea in my artistic life. I am an adapter. I look at something and get an idea of how I can do that myself — differently, my way, whatever — and I follow up, and it's a different work of art. The idea for knitting rag rugs was triggered by discovering some women who were weaving rugs from clothing rejected by the local thrift shop. Should I *not* be knitting rugs because I did not come up with the pure idea in a vacuum? Should no one else work with recycled clothing as raw material because they got there first? But we didn't get there first; women have been recycling textiles since the day after we invented textiles. I can only wonder what it would be like to have "pure" ideas. Don't worry about it. If this book gives you an idea, go for it. Your rug will be your own creation, no matter where the idea came from.

CHAPTER 1

Materials
The Heart of a Fabric Rug

To get started knitting fabric rugs, you don't need a lot, and you probably have most of it already. Furthermore, it won't cost very much at all to buy anything else you need. Here are the basics: a space to work in, raw material (old clothing), a way to cut clothing into fiber strips, processed fiber (so you can start knitting when inspiration strikes), a way to store your fiber/stash so you can find it easily, and needles that feel good in your hands.

A Space to Work In

Let's start by talking about studios: art-making spaces. You can't make art unless you have the materials at hand to make it from. And you need a place to store those materials. You don't get an idea, go to the store to buy parts, and come home and make your project — at least not when you're 30 miles from the store and working in recycled material anyway. I have a business license to make and sell rugs in my home and am fortunate to be able to give over one small bedroom in my 1,400-square-foot house to textile stash.

Having this studio matters a lot to me. I know that not everyone can afford to dedicate this much space to a craft, however, and fabric inventory can become a real challenge.

The solution to this challenge is to find some way to organize your growing stash. When I first started knitting rugs, I brought used clothing home, washed it, and stuffed it into pillowcases ready for processing. This worked well enough for a while, until I suddenly realized my house could be featured in a show about hoarding. It was not pretty. So I emptied all the pillowcases out, sorted the clothing into two *huge* piles (mostly tops and bottoms), and started processing each garment by cutting away the seams, button bands, and so on, until I had rough-shaped pieces that could be folded and stored more efficiently (what I call "flat fold"). I reduced the volume significantly by throwing away the parts that aren't useful for knitting.

Organization Has Influence

In her book *KnitKnit,* Sabrina Gschwandtner quotes Debbie New as saying, "The way you choose to arrange your yarns exerts some influence on what you choose to make with them." I completely agree! I need stash on hand and variety, and I need to be able to choose among a number of options and have the best one on hand. Raw material for these rugs is usually not found in a store, and living where I do, one plans trips to town carefully. Stash itself makes design decisions.

The Raw Materials

Most of my rugs are made from used clothes cut into long strips of woven or knitted fiber. I also sometimes use household linens (sheets and napkins), and sometimes purchased yard goods. You can find usable fabric in a lot of places.

Where to Find Fabric

YARD SALES. Visit yard sales, especially multifamily events. Show up toward the end of the morning and make an offer on "everything left over." Arrive with a great big truck to take everything. Note that you may be competing with local thrift shops, who may have made prior arrangements with the vendors. Craigslist or an equivalent is a similar source.

THRIFT SHOPS. Thrift shops in my part of the world have "bag days" or "dollar tables," when you can buy a bag full of clothing for $1 or less. Learn when these are scheduled, and plan to arrive either early or late; some thrift shops allow you to take everything left at the end of the day for even less money. (Incidentally, much of the clothing rejected by thrift shops is sold by the truckload to aggregators who ship it to developing countries, where it is processed and woven into rag rugs, which are then sold back to us at discount stores.) Look for "rag bags," and buy one to see what kinds of clothing get put into a rag bag. Some shops sort their rag bags by white or colored T-shirts. Pick the colored ones. These garments are likely to be stained and torn, but you may be able to cut around the ruined parts and still get a reasonable amount of fiber for the money.

YOUR FRIENDS. Tell your friends that you need old clothing, and that you don't care what shape it's in. I often come home to find bags of clothing on my doorstep.

TRASH/GARBAGE/DUMP. Where I live, we take our trash to a transfer station, and the county picks it up from there and takes it to the dump. Each transfer station has a swap shed, where people leave unwanted stuff that still has useful life. Much of this stuff is clothing. The swap sheds have provided me with more incoming fiber than I can knit.

HOME SEWERS' LEFTOVERS. A source I didn't consider until well into this project was my own stash of leftover fabrics from years of making clothes. All of those bits that were too big to throw away but too small to use for anything significant can be sliced into usable strips for knitting. Consider putting a small notice up in any fabric store in your area.

Unfortunately, much of the fabric used for quilt making and most upholstery fabric is printed on one side only. If the backside has strong color (solids), you can use it. If the backside looks like the backside (that is, not as bright or colorful as the front),

it's best to leave those pieces for a quilter. It has taken me several years to refine my input stream so that I no longer bring home very many garments or fabrics that don't work well. I used to actually iron yards of rayon strips so that the colorful side faced out, and the less-bright side was on the inside. I don't do that anymore. Nothing comes into the stash unless it has good color on both sides of the fabric. It doesn't have to be the same color on both sides, but it has to be useful.

Synthetics to Avoid

Although I do use polyesters and microfibers, there are some synthetics I won't touch.

- SPANDEX, LYCRA, MYLAR, AND FABRICS WITH GLITTER. I don't use anything that rots, and this includes spandex, Lycra, and Mylar. You know what happens to elastic that goes bad? The same thing happens with spandex, Lycra, and other high-percentage synthetic fabrics. By the time they're in the recycle stream, they may be just about to collapse. I've seen a few places in my rugs "go poppy," and I could have predicted this from the fiber content in the first place.

- LINGERIE. Some nightwear nylons are similar to the stretchy fabrics.

They tend to have great sheen, glimmer, and interesting colors, but they disintegrate over time. Stay away.

- ACETATE. I never use acetate, which is often used to line skirts and pants. Although it comes in good colors, acetate unfortunately dissolves completely in acetone (nail polish remover). My rugs might be used in a bathroom, where someone might spill nail polish remover, and I don't like the idea of a great big hole opening up in a rug. If you're not sure whether a lining fabric is acetate or polyester, put a drop of nail polish remover onto the fabric. If it's acetate, you'll be able to poke your finger through the wet place.

What to Collect

I apply several criteria to the garments that come into my house:

- Fiber source
- Garment construction and size
- Color

FIBER SOURCES

NATURAL FIBERS. I prefer natural fibers and blends, including cotton, wool, silk, and blends of all of these. I'm not a fiber purist. Many polo shirts and T-shirts are cotton-poly blends, and they work just fine. Although T-shirts are usually great, those with large plastic appliqués may not knit as smoothly as all-cotton shirts in solid colors. If you have an all-natural approach to life and art, feel free to restrict yourself to these kinds of fiber. You will be able to honor your values and still make knitted rugs.

SYNTHETICS (POLYESTER, MICRO-FIBERS, AND SO ON). Inexpensive brides-maids' and prom dresses are often made of polyester fabric. These garments have oodles of fabric, especially if the skirt is full, and they come in great colors. Knit polyester fabrics don't hold up as well as wovens, however. Also, the chiffonlike overlays used on some dresses have not turned out to be useful. Chiffon unravels, but cutting on the bias helps. The unraveled bits get all nasty and matted up when the rug gets washed a few years down the road, which is a pity, because I'd like to make use of their colors.

BURN TESTS

If you're not sure what something is made of, you can do a burn test on it. There are many kinds of burn tests, but here are the basics. Do this test over a sink, and take care that there is nothing in the area, such as a curtain or towel, that might catch fire accidentally.

Cut a small piece of fabric, long enough to hold safely without burning your fingers. Use a match to light the swatch on fire, then quickly blow it out.

- Cotton flares, burns cleanly, and smells like paper.
- Rayon flares, burns cleanly, and smells like paper.
- Silk and wool smell like hair.
- Polyester and other synthetics melt as fast as they burn, leave a little bead of plastic on the edge, and smell like chemistry.

GARMENT CONSTRUCTION

The garment that provides the perfect raw material for rug knitting is a seamless, extra-large T-shirt. You can cut a 50-yard strip of rug fiber from one shirt. Unfortunately, seamless extra-large T-shirts are only a small percentage of the recycle stream. You don't have to limit yourself to them, but knowing they are the acme of the search helps you understand what you're looking for. Here are some features to consider.

BIG PIECES. In general, the larger the garment, the longer the strip you'll be able to cut from it. Look for men's shirts, adult-size pants and trousers, full skirts (especially peasant skirts, once you cut out the gathered seams), and full-skirted dresses. Polo shirts are good, but be sure to cut out the extra button on the inside seam before slicing the garment into strips.

FEW SEAMS. Don't cut across seams when you cut a garment into strips, as the seams are likely to pull apart after the rug is completed. I learned this the hard way! Women's shirts are often made with lots of finicky bits, and by the time you cut out all the seams, there's nothing left. Fancy women's blouses, as well as dresses, are sometimes more trouble than they are worth. Jackets and suit coats have remarkably little useful material. Given that a decent used jacket, sports coat, or suit coat may help someone get a job, I don't pick these up unless they are ruined by stains or moth holes. Then, the backs can be used and sometimes the lining. Baby clothes are too small to bother with. They are also highly valued by families with low incomes, so don't hog the flow. Donate them back to a thrift shop.

OTHER CONSIDERATIONS. I don't use terry cloth or sweater knits. The fibers slub off, make a mess, and leave the remaining fabric thinner than you planned on.

The Search for Useful Colors

In chapter 2, you'll find information about color theory and designing with color, but this section contains advice that I hope will help you think in terms of color as you begin to collect fabrics and organize your stash.

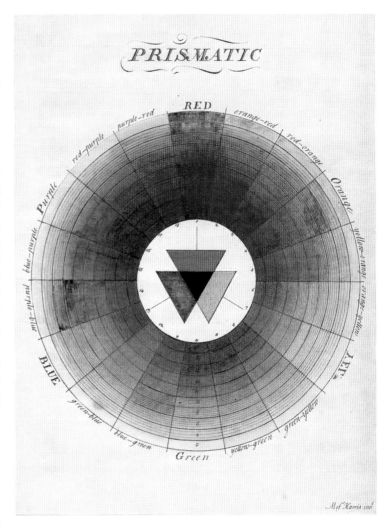

Moses Harris illustrated the first chart of Newton's color wheel.

RED. I can always work with anything on the red side of the color wheel: warm reds, cool reds, anything from maroon up to red-orange. Lighter than that goes to pink, which itself shades into peach. Peach is a very easy-to-live-with color. Usually it's easy to find reds in many garments, especially women's clothing and T-shirts. I've found that all reds run when wet, no matter what you do to them, so don't use a red rug against a surface that can stain.

ORANGE. Orange starts up at peachy and goes all the way down into the warmer browns. Frequently, you'll find orange as a fluorescent, which is tricky to use in home décor. Plenty of T-shirts and polo shirts show up in orange, often with stains that have to be cut out.

YELLOW. Clear yellow is a hard color to work with, because it draws a lot of attention to itself. It also gets dirty and stains easily. If you want to use a lot of yellow in a rug, it might be better to consider it wall art. Mustards are magic and play well with everything else, but they are hard to find in the recycled stream, though sometimes you'll find mustard-colored bed sheets.

GREEN. Greens can be warm or cool, yellow- or blue-based. Both sides work pretty well with turquoise and teal. Olive goes with everything. In my opinion, kelly green is death on a stick when it comes to blending. It's just plain ugly, and nothing plays well with it. Unfortunately, it's popular for soccer jerseys, school and band uniforms, and T-shirts, so you're likely to run

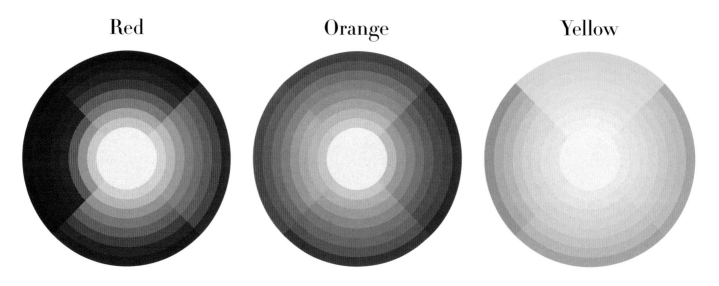

Red   Orange   Yellow

across it often. Electric lime and chartreuse can go nicely with some other colors. There are lots of massively useful sages, olives, and pines. You'll likely find green uniform pants, men's pants, and some T-shirts and polo shirts. Greens subsort into categories very quickly in my experience, and it can be difficult to accumulate enough of any one of the subcategories. Collect all the green you can find (except for that nasty kelly green, which, IMO, has no redeeming social value).

BLUE. I sometimes have trouble with blue. Not all blues — anything blue-green is fine. It's the dusty blues down to navy that stymie me. I don't like them, and they don't readily go with anything. My definition of "blue" is broad, and the blue colors I like to use overlap into green quite a bit: lapis, sapphire, royal blue, turquoise, teal.

VIOLET. Purple covers a broad spectrum, from more red to more blue, light to dark on both sides. They're all good, and they all play well with everything else. You do need to be able to distinguish between red-purple and blue-purple. Don't try this under artificial light. There isn't enough purple to suit me in the recycle stream. I collect all of it I can find, even the school uniforms and band pants. Darker purples hide stains well and work well on the floor. Be aware, however, that some purples will run in the wash.

Green   Blue   Violet

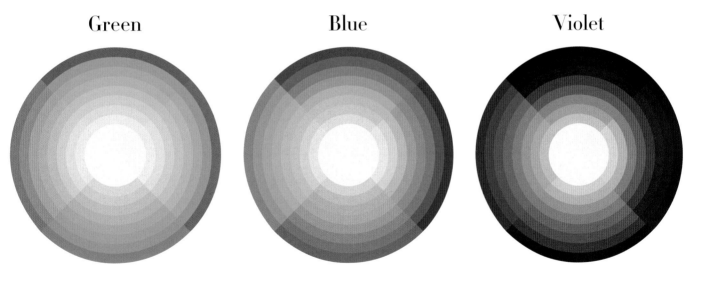

Good Color Blenders

BROWNS. I was on rug number 40 when I got a commission to make a set of rugs in a particular colorway that set me to collecting beiges and khakis. Wow-iola! What a great gift! All the colors of men's pants — khaki, beige, dun, tan, gray. These are all subtle, fabulous blending colors, and I suggest you collect them from the start. I'm a big fan of brights — primaries and secondaries — but the blenders make a rug easy to live with.

GRAY. Grays are good to keep on hand, but they can be difficult to use unless you're working with black. Grays often have a blue cast, which makes them hard to pair with some of the warmer colors. That said, grays tend to be useful. Lots of T-shirts are the same basic gray, shifted only by dye lot and washing habits.

BLACK AND WHITE. Black and white are striking, but hard to live with as an interior color scheme. If your children or grandchildren drink grape-colored drinks, do not use a black-and-white rug on the floor.

Grays often prove to be useful as color blenders.

The Day I Kicked Navy Out of My Stash

There was a bit of a panic in the rug room. I couldn't fit any more blue into its legal-sized, lateral file drawer. I yanked it all out, realized the drawer was half full of navy and a lot of the less fabulous blues, and decided to (a) get rid of what I had on hand and (b) not bring any more home. As it happened, there was a load in the dryer that I didn't have room for, three laundry baskets waiting to be sliced, and two more full black trash bags waiting to go into those baskets. Incoming was gaining on me. Why then would I want to bring home anything that wasn't actually fabulous, or at least interesting?

Blues are hard (for me) in a way that no other color is difficult. I don't like the color of denim jeans. It doesn't go with anything but red, pink, black, and white. There are other reasons to ban denim from knitted rugs: it's usually a different color on the wrong side, it's a bear to cut, it's hard to cut thin enough strips to marry with other fabrics, it's likely to stain wooden needles, and it's hard on razor wheels. With all of this against denim, I made an artist's decision: no more denim blue, and no oxford-cloth blue, or navy either. I knit out as much of it as I could in two final blue rugs and gave away the rest at a rug-knitting class. This is a scary decision. What if people suddenly stop leaving clothes at the swap shed? Then I might need all those blues!

You may hate other colors. I hereby give you permission to hate any color you want, and I recommend that you not use it. Keep in mind, however, that some colors that you dislike may be useful in some situations. Khaki, for instance, is easy to hate and, at the same time, the most useful color on the palette for an interior space. If you do collect denim, find a way to create an even blend of tweedy colors. Including fabric from only one or two pairs of jeans in a project will give a blocky look to your colorway.

Washing Raw Materials

Everything that comes into my house, from any source, gets cold-water washed and machine-dried to "bake." One important reason to do this is to ensure that the fabric has shrunk as much as it's going to, even though most used clothing has been machine washed and dried to maximum shrinkage long before it gets to the recycle stream. I use cold water, because hot water washing is expensive, and let machine drying take care of any remaining shrinkage. Decorator fabrics, particularly curtains, may never have been washed before, so they may need more than one trip through the dryer to reach maximum shrinkage. I don't use dryer sheets or any scented laundry products.

As mentioned previously, reds always run. Always. Many blues do, too. I'm thinking of a beautiful set of cotton curtains I found once, labeled "Made in Pakistan." They bled blue through several washings and dryings. If you face that sort of challenge, be sure never to put a rug with colors that won't stop bleeding on top of a cream Berber or other light-colored carpet.

When clothing comes out of the dryer, I stack it as flat as reasonable, by type. Pants get folded flat, seams to the sides (not creased). Shirts get stacked, roughly flat. The fewer folding creases you can insert into the garments at this stage, the easier it will be to cut the clothing later.

Estimating How Much Fabric You Need

Cut some fabric, such as a T-shirt (or two or three), into 1-inch strips. I call this "slicing." (For an illustration of how to most efficiently cut up a T-shirt, see page 18.) Pick a pair of needles, perhaps a pair in the US double-digit ranges (US 10 or 10.5, for example), but it's up to you. Cast on six or eight stitches with one strip, and knit in garter stitch for a few rows (knit every row). See what you get. See how your hands feel. If your hands hurt or if they are giving hints that they may hurt soon, increase needle size. If the sample is too skimpy, and you think it won't hold up to foot traffic, use smaller needles so that the fabric will be thicker.

When you're happy with the result, measure the length and width of the resulting swatch and multiply those two figures to get the area of the swatch in square inches. Then, unravel the swatch and measure the length of the fabric strip you used to knit it. When you decide the measurements for the rug you'd like to knit, again multiply length by width to calculate the rug's total area. Divide that figure by the area of the swatch to get the number of swatch area units in the finished rug. Then, multiply that result by the number of yards of fabric strips you used in your swatch. This is the measurement of the strips you have to slice and tie up in order to get close to the size of the planned project. I usually estimate 60 yards per square foot of finished rug.

The actual result is a bit less, but it's better to have more than you need.

(For information on how to calculate yardage for circular rugs, see page 138.)

It's important to keep the stitch count per piece or section low, because the overriding variable in rug knitting with recycled fabric is *weight*. These rugs get *heavy*, quickly. If the project requires straight sides (rectangular sections), I don't like to have more than 14 stitches on a 10" needle. I can fit and hold up to 17 stitches on a 10" needle, so if I'm knitting a square on the diagonal, my modules tend to be 17 stitches at their widest. At approximately 1½ to 2 stitches to the inch, this makes them no wider than 11½ inches. I sometimes use 14" needles to increase the maximum width of a diagonally knitted square up to 22 or 23 stitches, but I can't hold a 14" needle with full rows of 22 stitches for long at all without causing

Sample Calculation for Estimating Fabric

MEASUREMENT OF SWATCH
12" × 12" = 1 square foot (*area of swatch*)

PLANNED MEASUREMENT OF RUG
3' × 4' = 12 square feet (*area of rug*)

NUMBER OF UNITS REQUIRED
12 square feet (*area of rug*) ÷ 1 square foot (*area of swatch*) = 12 (*swatch units*)

MEASUREMENT OF FABRIC STRIPS USED TO KNIT SWATCH
60 yards

TOTAL YARDAGE NEEDED FOR RUG
12 units × 60 yards (*fabric strip measurement*) = 720 yards of fabric strips needed for 3' × 4' rug

pain in my wrist and elbows. After 8 or 10 rows, I decrease enough to fit all the stitches on the smaller needle and switch back to 10" needles.

I have not found a large-gauge circular needle that works for me, although I am a fan of circulars when I'm knitting something other than rugs. The limitation imposed by 10" double-pointed needles has a certain design value for me in itself. I might never have investigated modular knitting, and from there quilt patterns and tessellations, if I had found a way to knit huge sections comfortably without breaking them down into more manageable modules.

- Project size depends on module size, and the number of modules required to yield a given final project size is a factor of gauge.
- It is much easier to knit with fiber that is cut to a consistent weight, because this allows you to knit at a consistent gauge.

WHY GAUGE DOESN'T MATTER. It's a rug. Does it really matter if it's an inch or 5 inches bigger or smaller than you thought it might be? If not, don't worry. Find a comfortable pair of needles, cast on, and go. It will all work out.

Does Stitch Gauge Matter?

It's easier to knit a rug once you learn how to cut your fiber so it mostly knits up to a fairly uniform stitch size. That said, I am a maverick on gauge (a specified number of stitches per inch). Telling someone to "knit to gauge" when you're talking about a rug is ridiculous. You knit what you knit and you get what you get. So on one hand, gauge doesn't matter, and on the other, it does. Here's why, and why not.

WHY GAUGE MATTERS. It is helpful, though not absolutely necessary, to know how much fiber it will take to finish a given project. (This assumes one is knitting recycled fabric with ready access to more, rather than buying new yarn from a limited supply.)

I usually use US 10 or 10.5 straight needles, 10 inches long.

Cutting Strips for Consistent Gauge

This is tricky: learning to cut fabrics of different weights so that they knit to something approximating a consistent gauge. It's all a matter of how wide to cut the strips. One method is to stick to T-shirts, which are roughly the same fabric weight, unless they are ancient and washed to death, but that leaves out all the fun of slicing up choir robes and old bridesmaids' dresses and stretch pants and polo shirts. In time, it's possible to develop a feel for gauge and get it right almost automatically. In the interim, there's a test to get it right. You'll need a knitting needle sizing gauge to do this. A drill-bit gauge will work as well.

Start with a piece of sliced fabric that feels good when you knit it on your preferred needles. Pull it through a few holes on your knitting gauge until you find a hole that it slides through reasonably easily without too much tugging, but not so fast that it doesn't stop at all. This is your target hole.

1. Cut a long triangle of the fabric you plan to knit with, about 3″ at the wide end, and 6″–8″ long.

2. Insert the pointed end through the hole in the knitting gauge two sizes *smaller* than your target. Pull the fabric through, but don't force it. Mark the fabric at the point it starts to stick in the hole. Pull it out of the gauge.

Next, pull the triangle through another hole, two sizes *larger* than the target. Again, mark where the fabric stops easily, without fighting it. (If it flows all the way through this hole, try a smaller target hole, or make a wider triangle.)

3. Run this test on each different weight of fabric selected for your project, until you learn to guesstimate accurately enough for your standards.

4. Smooth out your fabric triangles. Note that you have a "too thin" mark and a "too wide" mark on each. The ideal width for your strips is the width of the triangle at about the midpoint between your two marks. Notice that the width of the strips you'd need for the red fabric is narrower than that for the blue, as the red fabric is a heavier weight.

Although you could also measure each strip of fabric as it is sliced, I do not do this. A little variety adds texture to my rugs. Also, speed is king when slicing.

1.

2.

3.

4.

Tools for Cutting

THE CUTTING MAT. Get the largest cutting mat you can find. It's much easier to use a large mat. Folding fabric and cutting multiple layers just to fit on a smaller mat gets stale very quickly. The biggest cutting mats cost approximately $100 at the larger sewing-supply stores. Look around to see if you can take advantage of a 40-percent-off coupon in the Sunday newspaper or on a smart phone app.

TABLE HEIGHT. Be good to yourself and get the ergonomics right for your slicing station. Slicing is a physically demanding activity, and it doesn't take much to generate serious back, shoulder, or hand pain. Slicing became much easier when I raised my table by putting 4-inch blocks under the legs. Shorter people may want to saw a few inches off their worktable's legs.

ROTARY CUTTER. Use a good rotary cutter, *not* scissors, for cutting fabric strips. If you use scissors, you will destroy your cutting hand in no time at all. Although I love my Gingher scissors and have a great sharpening service, I use scissors and shears only for roughing out garments, trimming, releasing long strips of fabric (see Cutting T-Shirts and Polo Shirts, page 22), and sometimes for taking collars off shirts. I do *not* use scissors or shears for cutting the long strips.

When cutting lightweight knit fabrics and worn-out T-shirts, I use a right-hand Martelli ErgoCutter model. The angled grip takes the strain off my wrist and allows my body to use upper-arm and shoulder muscles, rather than wrist and forearm muscles, to guide the cut. The grip also allows me to keep the blade more perpendicular to the cutting surface, which reduces wear on the blade edge.

When I first saw the Martelli advertised, my body recognized its value before my mind did. Traditional rotary cutters don't make it easy to cut on the return stroke, so each yard of cut is effectively two yards of shoulder and elbow motion. Even so, I debated whether a new piece of equipment would be sufficiently different to be worth it. Now that I've been using it, I don't hesitate to say that this cutter is worth the money. I can cut for hours at a stretch and also cut on the pull or return stroke, doubling my slicing efficiency. The edge lasts longer, slicing 40 to 60 garments before it needs sharpening, compared to 20 garments with an ordinary cutter.

I also use a low-end model of the Jiasew electric fabric cutter. This tool cuts woven and substantial knits much better than it cuts slinky knits. The Jiasew cuts 8 to 12 layers of sheet-weight fabric in one pass, and 4 to 8 layers of heavier fabric. Please understand that this is a dangerous tool intended for professional use. It will remove fingers. Do not use it if children have access to your cutting table.

Although the cutting machines used to cut wool strips for hooked rugs might seem like another option for slicing, the widest strip you can cut with these tools is ¼" and I usually need about ¾". These machines are also quite expensive.

SHARPENERS. Whatever tool you choose for cutting, be sure to keep it sharp. And oh, the joy of finding a good sharpening service! Newly sharpened Gingher shears cut six layers of upholstery fabric effortlessly. No matter how good an edge someone puts on a blade, however, entropy wins in the end. The hard, rough work of processing clothing into knitting fiber is one of the more challenging uses of scissors and blades.

I invested in a blade sharpener for my rotary blades when I discovered they cost $5 each (a little less for a pack of 50). I use the Dritz model. I can get about four sharpenings per blade, which reduces the effective cost to $1 per blade and pays for the sharpener in four blades' worth of cutting.

Safety Considerations

All textile work is dusty. Because tearing fabric generates more dust than cutting, I prefer cutting, but even winding the cut strips is a very linty operation. I spread a sheet over the furniture to catch the threads that fall everywhere, use a room-size air filter, keep the window open whenever possible or point a fan so that it blows air away from my face, and wear a dust mask. Also, I installed an 1800 CFM whole-house fan in the attic, which keeps a constant airflow drawing over my work surface. When neither the heating nor air-conditioning systems are in use, this fan provides good ventilation. I've taken these precautions because I work with textiles in such quantities. Use your own judgment about what makes sense for you — and listen to your sneezes!

In addition to health considerations, you'll soon discover that your workroom, including light fixtures, is covered with lint, so you'll need to vacuum regularly. Lint is flammable! Clean the lint filter in your clothes dryer twice as often once you start processing clothing for rug making. Most house fires start with the dryer. Don't take chances.

Preparing Fabrics for Cutting

By strategizing your approach to cutting garments apart, you'll be able to maximize the length of useful strips for your knitting. Different garments require slightly different approaches.

Cutting T-Shirts and Polo Shirts

A T-shirt is the ideal garment to slice. Many T-shirts have no seams in the body, and the fabric is a good weight for knitting. The colors tend to be bold.

ROUGH CUTS. Begin by cutting off and discarding the hem and sleeve bands. Next, cut three sections — one from the body, and one from each sleeve — then cut off the top portion of the yoke on both front and back, eliminating the neck ribbing. Discard the rest of the yoke.

X =piece to discard

CUTTING THE STRIPS. If you are lucky enough to be working with a T-shirt that has no side seams, lay the shirt out flat and begin cutting across the shirt, parallel to where the bottom hem was. (To determine the width of your strips, see Cutting Strips for Consistent Gauge, page 18.) Stop your cut 2″ short of the fold on the opposite side (A).

Make another cut parallel to the first, again stopping short of folded edge on the other side. Continue to make parallel cuts up the entire body of the shirt, always starting on the same side and stopping short of the opposite side edge.

To release a long fabric strip, open the tube, and starting at the bottom edge on the side of the shirt that is still

A.

joined, cut the first strip on a diagonal toward the slit that begins the second strip (B). Continue up the shirt, releasing each strip by cutting diagonally across the side section that you left uncut in step A. When you reach the top, you will have released the entire body in one long continuous strip (C).

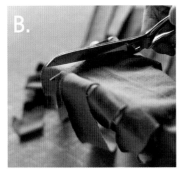

An alternative to releasing the strips with scissors is to lay the fringed, unreleased tube on a narrow cutting board and slice with a rotary razor. In the photos at the right, the body of the shirt is resting on a sleeve board, protected with a strip of cutting mat. It can be a little bit quicker to release large sections of fabric with a rotary cutter than with scissors, but I often use scissors to snip the last tiny bit at the end of a long pass made with a rotary cutter before I start back in the opposite direction (A, B, C).

You can gain a few more yards by slicing the upper body of the shirt zigzag fashion, above the lower edge of the armholes (D). Make your cuts from one side to the other, always stopping about 1″ short of the edge. Depending on the bulk of the sleeve seams, I may

or may not trim them away. If you don't trim them beforehand, when you get to the neck, trim off the front piece, unfold the top, and keep going. You

may need to snip the neck at center front to allow the fabric to lie flat.

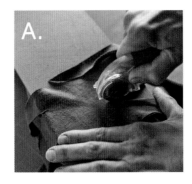

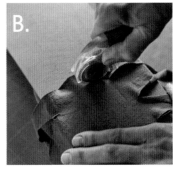

Cutting Button-Front Shirts

Button-front shirts are a bit more challenging. Start with the sleeves, cutting them up in this order: first cut off the cuffs, then take the sleeves off the body, and finally trim the seam off the sleeves. Then, slice the remaining fabric into strips by cutting zigzag fashion lengthwise as described for T-shirts.

To prepare the body, cut off the button and button-hole bands and the collar, then trim off the bottom (if the shirt has tails), and cut off the upper portion at the base of the armholes. This leaves a large rectangle that can be zigzag sliced into one long strip. You can probably get another strip from the upper back, and sometimes from the two upper front pieces. If the shirt has a double yoke, the shoulders may need to be sliced half-width, or simply discarded.

⊗ =piece to discard   – – – =cut to remove

↕ =direction of zigzag slices

buttons break blades!

Cutting Pants, Skirts, and Dresses

For pants, discard the seams, then cut strips by zigzagging up and down the length of the leg. It's important to make lengthwise strips; if you slice in a spiral around a pant leg, you'll have a seam every six or eight inches, which is undesirable. Skirts and dresses may be sliced spiral fashion around the garment or lengthwise, depending on whether there are seams.

⊗ =piece to discard

– – – =cut to remove

↕ =direction of zigzag slices

watch out for hardware!

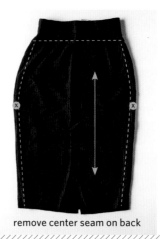

remove center seam on back

Storing the Fabric Strips

When a basket or two is full of sliced garments, I stop and wind the strips into balls, keeping same-colored fabric from each garment together. At this point, I don't tie the ends together, but simply tuck them into the ball as the fiber is wound. I discard any strips shorter than 3 feet long and start a new ball when one gets to about 5 inches in diameter. I like to wind balls while I'm talking on the phone or watching a movie on TV. It doesn't take the same amount of attention and thought as making color selections.

Sort the rolled balls of fiber by color. As you accumulate fabric stash, store your materials in an organized way. Lateral file cabinets hold a lot of fiber and keep it reasonably accessible. (The backs of traditional front-to-back file cabinet drawers aren't as easy to see or reach into.)

Translucent, lidded plastic storage containers also hold a reasonable amount of fiber, and they are stackable. Plus, you can see through the sides to get some idea of what's in them. I organize and store the balls by their predominant color.

Select a storage system that packs well, so that it will stand up to your growing stash. Cheap containers that fall over easily will prove to be more trouble than they are worth. Cardboard boxes attract damp and insects and have a higher acid content than is safe for fibers.

For longer-term storage, vacuum bags that compress loose material will gain you some space. The small ones are travel sized and use body weight to generate compression. Larger ones require a household vacuum cleaner to pull the air out of the bag, creating a more compact package. One shortcoming of vacuum storage is that it's not possible to control the final shape of the compressed package. Vacuum storage bags last a great deal longer if they are stored in a smooth, safe outer container, such as a hard-sided plastic bin, where a nail or splinter can't poke a hole through the plastic and destroy the seal.

You won't gain as much space using compression if you're loading the bag with flat-fold cloth, rather than rolled balls of processed fiber. Nonetheless, the fiber is protected from humidity and insects until ready for use. If you store the package out of the sun, it will also be protected from fading.

CHAPTER 2

Color!

Rules of Thumb

While many books send artists to color wheels for inspiration, I have not found them helpful. The 8 or 16 colors in a traditional color wheel just aren't enough to feed my imagination. Quiltmaker Freddy Moran said it best: "Ten colors don't work; 100 colors do." A color wheel gives you 10 colors; a paint-selection book gives you 100.

Sometimes my color choices are completely arbitrary. For instance, I might pull colors from my stash when a drawer gets too full. "The red drawer won't close. Better use up some red today." Then, what goes with red? (Everything.) But I also use a variety of sources for inspiration, as well as some simple rules of thumb, such as, "White is not a color" and "Everything looks better with black." Here are some other suggestions that come from my experience.

COMMIT TO A COLORWAY. That will get you out of a rut when your first rug doesn't thrill you. Collect tons and tons of fabrics in your choice of colors, then play around with them as much as you want. Begin your experiments by playing on paper. Or if you can work with digital photographs and such software as Photoshop Elements, you may want to try cutting and pasting images of existing rugs to see what a new pattern might look like.

USE COLORS PURPOSEFULLY. Think about how you want your colors to be balanced. Do you want the design to move from one big color area to another? Or do you want a fairly even balance of your colors throughout the rug? You may or may not decide also to have a focal point in the pattern. The overall pattern of the rug should work with the room, and it's even possible that the rug itself will be the focal point of the room.

Inspired by Color

There are a wide variety of places to find inspiration for color and color combinations. My favorite sources of color inspiration are, in order, the *Pantone Guide to Communicating with Color* by Leatrice Eiseman, my personal collection of pages torn from shelter magazines (particularly the ads), and *The Home Color Selector,* by David Willis, in association with Benjamin Moore Paints. I have developed my awareness of color and its possibilities by reading several other Pantone books by Leatrice Eiseman, authors like Freddy Moran and Gwen Marston, Kaffe Fassett, and Jinny Beyer (especially *Color Confidence for Quilters).* Here are some other possibilities for finding color inspiration.

Paint Chips

Every so often, the major paint companies refresh their swatch suggestions at the big hardware stores. You can get some starting-point ideas from these color cards, although most are pretty tame, even the ones that are intended to be extreme. Home-decorating paint books are also good sources of color. The trick is to use *all* the colors they recommend putting together, not just one set of accents and secondary colors. I especially love those paint chips with the cut-out that lets you see another color chip placed below it.

Magazine Pages

Years ago, I collected colored pages out of magazines and made collages of interesting colors, and now have color combinations enough to keep me in ideas until the end of time. Now, I simply leaf through a magazine, find a picture that I like, identify the major colors in it, and throw in enough extra colors and shades from my stash to get to 100 or thereabouts. Once the major tones are identified, I shift to finding 15 shades of olive, or 25 warm reds (light to dark), or 5 peaches. When you see models in magazine pictures, look at the areas of skin and hair as color blocks, too. You'll see peaches, oranges, and browns. These are part of what attracted you to the image in the first place, and you need to include these colors in your work if you want it to sing the way the picture did for you. Unfortunately, I have not been able to capture with photography the colors I find attractive in objects and scenes around me. I find swatches on paper, paint chips, and using colored pencils more helpful.

Printed Fabric

Printed fabric is a great source of color suggestions. Rayons are usually the best. If you don't want an exact copy (which you can't get, because those are prints, and you're going to be knitting), change the proportion of colors. Try using a lot of a color that is only a tiny accent in your inspiration fabric. Pink and Yellow Log Cabin rug (page 96) was inspired by a swatch of rayon fabric.

I find a lot of inspiration in Sam Hilu and Irwin Hersey's book *Bogolanfini Mud Cloth*. Although the dramatic fabric patterns in this book are (somewhat obviously) in the colors of . . . mud, and used clothing is rarely brown, I can see these patterns in bright red and black just fine. Just looking at the designs in this book sets my mind to rambling. When you stare at a pattern that's printed in strong, bold, contrasting colors, and you are a rug knitter, before long you start wondering how to make that pattern work in garter stitch and discover that many of these patterns can be knit.

Quilt Patterns

When I look over my rugs and ask myself where the original idea for each rug came from, it's quilt patterns, especially patchwork squares, that get the most points. When I first began knitting rugs, I checked all the patchwork books out of the library and pasted pages from my patch-a-day calendar into my sketchbook. Eventually, I was able to analyze the patterns in art quilts and draw ideas from their general structure, especially the interplay of color that could be reinterpreted in garter stitch units.

When you research patchwork quilts, look for patterns with square sides, or with 60- or 90-degree angles. These shapes can

Most of the squares in this mud cloth sample can be knit in garter stitch. (The polka dots are tricky!)

be knit, whereas it's harder to knit curves. Some patterns, including some log cabin designs, have an arrangement that looks like curves but can be made to work. One of my favorite sources is Karen Combs's *Celtic Pieced Illusions*. Most quilts built on Celtic designs are appliqué, rather than pieced blocks, but Ms. Combs shows how to build a fabulous interlaced quilt design using only two basic squares, both of which can be easily knitted in garter stitch.

The downside of relying too heavily on quilt books is that patchworkers are able to work tiny — one or two inches on a side — then use many squares to create a very rich surface. As you knit with fabric strips, you'll very quickly learn what it means to work at 2 stitches to the inch, and that four squares of a quilt block is plenty when you're transposing that design into your knitted rug.

Other needlework books may offer ideas as well. For instance, you can knit most Bargello patterns by managing long stripes with color changes.

Selecting Colors for a New Rug

When it's time to prepare fiber for a new rug, I pull out as many balls of color as could possibly work into the rug I have in mind. I work and adjust and shift things around and go back to my stash for more, until I'm happy with my colorways.

I sometimes think of a group of colors as telling a color "story." For instance, the basic colorway I call November consists of browns and grays. When I decided to knit a rug using this colorway, I first went through my stash to get out all the browns and tans. I can do a first sort in the evening by lamplight but always do the final selection under natural daylight (in a room with a solar tube

Disclaimer: Colors to Hate

I recommend that you find a handful of colors to hate and promise you'll never use. It makes life a little more interesting. At the same time, you'll find that possibly, just possibly, you may need some of these colors one day. I learned something about this in a color class I took at the University of North Carolina's continuing education program. The four colors I chose to hate were two insipid pinks that looked something like watery Pepto-Bismol, one kelly-ish green, and a wishy-washy sky blue. The next week's assignment was to find colors that made these colors work.

The large blue, pink, and green paint chips shown here represent the base colors I really couldn't stand. The green never came in, but adding browns made the pink and blue acceptable.

skylight). If your access to natural light is limited, you may be able to do some color work with an OttLite, which features natural-light LED illumination.

Choosing Accent Colors

Sorting the predominant color from light to dark is fairly straightforward. It's the tweedy bits of accent colors that can be challenging. If you choose a main color in a home paint book, you may find that the book also contains suggestions for four sets of accent colors that go well with that main color. If you want your textile work to really sing, use *all* of the accent colors suggested for that one main color. *The Home Color Selector* offers three pages of "base" colors, with four sets of four accent colors on each base, for a total of 48 suggested accents. I use them all. If 80 percent of a project is one color — for example, brown — then 20 percent can be everything else that goes

well with brown, as long as it's the same value (see Use Red Lenses to Sort Colors into Shades, page 32). Sophisticated colorists are able to look at these accent colors and realize that they're actually not all that different from each other. While this is true, they're different enough that if you use all 48 of the suggested colors, your rug will sing in a way that using one base plus four accents can never achieve.

The real challenge here is to avoid the "matchy-matchy" syndrome. Have you ever looked at a quilt made from a package of selected fabrics, all from one designer's fabric line? No matter how lively, you can always tell it was made from a kit. All the colors match just a little too closely. (Mixing in some silk is one way of getting more life in a quilt — or a rug — and fabrics that have a shiny look also help solve the "matchy-matchy" problem.)

The assortment of neutrals at the left is brought to life with the carefully chosen accent colors at the right.

As mentioned, my single most-used color guide is Leatrice Eiseman's *Pantone Guide to Communicating with Color*, especially when I'm choosing accent colors. Any and all colors on each page will play well with every other color on the page. Pick a handful to be the main colors in a work, and use all of the others as sparkly bits, accents, and secondaries. You won't go wrong.

Use Red Lenses to Sort Colors into Shades

Once the accent colors are selected, I sort them by shade, or value. Value is the way we describe where a color sits on a scale from light to dark. When you're working with color, it can be difficult to tell exactly how light or dark it is, because the human eye gets distracted by the color. "Is this gray brighter than this green, or not?"

One of the most useful tools you can get as a designer is a pair of red-tinted glasses or a piece of red acetate. (Orange or pink lenses will do in a pinch. I've even successfully used a transparent pink plastic spoon.) Red glasses take the color out of the world, leaving only the various shades of what is called the gray scale: the white-to-black, lightness-to-darkness of an object. Red lenses are an invaluable tool when sorting and selecting color. They do such a good job of pinpointing a value that is out of harmony with its neighbors that when you take the glasses off, you may even have trouble finding the missorted color.

If you can get colors and values sorted and aligned, your design work will be much more powerful. You could achieve the same

results by taking a black-and-white picture, but it's easier to take the glasses off, rearrange the colors as necessary, then check again with the glasses than it is to take a picture and try to work off the screen with my phone's camera.

Many designers use a 1–10 system, in which 1 is pure white and 10 is pure black. When you design, it helps if you make a conscious decision about where you are playing in this world. It's fine to stay in a 4–7 or 3–6 range, but your rug will be better if you have made that decision consciously, rather than defaulted to it because you didn't think to add an extreme at either end. (For instance, what do you think about 1, combined with 4–9?) Experiment with your color ideas on paper with colored pencils to see what they look like. This is far easier than knitting up your color concepts.

Once I've sorted my colors by value, I put everything that's one shade in a plastic bag and label it: light red into one bag, for instance, and dark red into another. It's important to label the shades, because if you knit in artificial light, it's very easy to get color shades mixed up.

Tying the Sorted Colors into Workable Balls

The final step before knitting is to tie up the different shades within each bag into several larger balls to knit from. Working from a bag that contains only one shade (say, light red), remove a strip from 3 to 6 feet

Without the distraction of color, it's easier to create a smooth transition in value from dark to light. Note how misplaced yarns pop out in the black-and-white version below.

long from one ball. (If a strip is longer, tear it into lengths no shorter than 3 feet. It's okay to use strips slightly longer than 6 feet, but less than 3 feet isn't useful.) Put that ball in an empty basket and take another ball from the plastic bag and remove a 3- to 6-foot strip from that one, too. Then, very loosely tie these two strips together with a square knot, leaving tails at least 6 inches long on each strip. (It's important to make loose knots at this point, because you may

have to untie them later when you are knitting.) You will be knitting these tails into the rug when you come to the knots, so the ends must be long enough to be knit into at least two stitches on either side of the knot. Continue to knot together strips from alternating balls of light red until you have used one strip from each ball. Repeat until you have 50–60 yards tied up. Wind the tied-together strips into new balls.

This is a good time to make a rough estimate of your yardage. A quick-and-dirty way to do this is to measure the width of your arm span, which is usually about the same as your height. You'll never be without a measuring stick if you keep this in mind. You may soon get so that you can estimate how much yardage is in one of your loosely wound balls just by feel. Run the fiber from hand to hand. For me, at 6 feet tall, one arm span is 2 yards.

Follow this procedure with each of the shades you bagged up. Label the balls as well. (One way to label them is shown on page 26.)

If you're anxious to get started knitting, you might want to tie up one ball of each of the colors you're using and come back later to tie up the rest. It's important to make a separate ball for each of the shades you are working with; that is, if a rug is knit from eight shades of a color, you should have eight bags of sorted fiber and at least eight balls, one of each shade, when you start knitting. This is what will give your rugs sparkle and variety. The more shades in each of the colors used in a rug, the more interesting it will be.

Black Is Not Black

Because I use black in all the rugs I knit, I keep balls of tied-up black ready to go. Because black varies, I like to mix blacks from different garments. I've found that if I knit a big patch of black from one garment into a design, it's quite noticeable. Blending the blacks, even though they may not look that different to you before knitting, gives a much richer effect.

CHAPTER 3

Process
Rug-Making Nuts and Bolts

If you have a pile of rag strips — inherited, purchased, or found at a yard sale — and you're just itching to cast on and knit, skip ahead to any of the patterns and go at it. You'll learn more by knitting than reading about it. Promise yourself you'll make a second rug if you're not happy with the first; that's how I got started. If you need a bit more background and like to understand what's going on before you commit, this chapter will help.

Making Your Paper Plan

As you'll see, throughout this book are examples from my notebooks, showing the development process of each of my designs. This is critically important. Every mistake I have ever had to unpick and do over (or live with) would have been avoided if I had spent more time on paper before I cast on. Every. Single. Mistake. Not only will it save you unpicking your work, but in-progress corrections are difficult to hide. Stay on paper longer!

An advantage of working in garter stitch is that each stitch is nearly square. Knitter's graph paper has rectangular units, because most knit stitches are wider than they are tall. Because you're dealing with garter stitch, however, you can work out your designs on regular graph paper. But you can get in trouble if you don't remain aware that, although garter stitch is more square than most other stitches, it's not completely square.

Scale is another thing to consider when you make your plans on paper. Things that look okay in a 4-inch-wide drawing will look very different when you knit them up to be 4 feet wide. Use big pieces of paper to finalize your designs so that you'll have a better idea how they'll hold up to enlargement.

When designing on paper, notice that the lines you create in the paper pattern are what will give your rug structure and pattern. The most obvious lines are those around the edges of the rug, but lines are also created where smaller units within the rug join. In addition, clear-cut color changes within the small units also form lines. Each of these is part of your design.

If you have doubts about the effectiveness of your paper design, test it by knitting a smaller rug first. If you don't like it, you'll find out in a shorter amount of time. Be willing to knit again.

When planning any rug, take into account how much time you want the project to take, how much fiber it will require, and how much the finished rug will weigh. For example, I considered making each of the 36 units of Blue and Black Log Cabin rug (page 102) bigger. Enlarging each of the units as little as 1 inch, however, would have made a big difference in each of those factors. Also, I have found that both the bright blues and the black-and-white blends used in that rug are reasonably rare in the recycled stream, so the smaller size was probably the right choice.

Casting On with Fabric Strips

When you cast on, start with a piece of fiber that's long enough to cast on all stitches without encountering a knot. (You'll need about four times the width of the cast on.) You may have to untie the first piece of fiber or two from your tied-up ball to find a useful cast-on piece.

I use the simplest of all cast ons: the knitted cast on. To do this, make a slip knot, leaving a 12- to 20-inch tail that you can use later to stitch pieces together, and place the slip knot on your left-hand needle. Insert the tip of your right-hand needle into the slip knot, as if you were going to knit it. Wrap the fabric strip under the tip of the right-hand needle from back to front, draw a loop through the slip knot, and place the new stitch on the left-hand needle, orienting the new stitch so that the front leg is in front of the back leg (see photo below). Continue to add new stitches in the same

For a knitted cast on, knit into the first stitch on the left-hand neeedle, then place the new stitch next to it.

way until you have the number indicated on the pattern. Take care not to pick up the tail and knit with it instead of the working strip!

Why Garter Stitch?

Garter stitch is what you get when you knit every row, in contrast to stockinette stitch, which is created by alternating knit and purl rows. As I mentioned in the introduction, I choose to knit my rugs in garter stitch because I find it difficult to purl when I'm using the large needles and fabric strips needed for rugs. It turns out that garter stitch is ideal for reasons other than comfort. The structure of the stitch makes for springier rugs, with a side-to-side stretch that is pretty much the same as its top-to-bottom stretch. ("Knit one below" would also result in a great super-dense rug, but you have to purl back, which for me doesn't work.) Also, as previously mentioned, a single garter stitch is almost square, which makes designing on traditional graph paper just a little bit easier. (If you cut your fabric strips so that you get a consistent gauge when you knit, you will get roughly the same number of stitches as rows per inch.)

The characteristic structure of garter stitch creates an effect that's important to keep in mind when you change colors: a clean, straight line forms between the previous row and the current one on the right side where you start the new color. If you turn the piece over, you'll see that on the other side, the line between the old and new colors is broken. I always change colors on what will be the right side of the rug. To help me remember where I am when I'm working, I place a marker on the front side of the piece I'm working on, and make all my color changes on that side. When you get into designs based on log cabin quilting patterns, it will be especially important to keep track of your right and wrong sides.

Even on rugs that have two right sides (the spirals and the shaded stripes), you'll be happier with your results if you knit to create a "right" side (solid-line color changes) and a "wrong" side (dotted-line color changes). Discerning eyes can tell the difference.

In garter stitch, changing color on the right side creates a smooth line (far left); on the wrong side (left), the same color change creates a dotted line.

Changing Colors and Counting Garter-Stitch Rows

CHANGING COLORS. Because color changes in garter stitch look different depending on whether the new color starts on the front or the back of the rug, it's important to pay attention to which side is up when changing colors. You may think that if you change colors on the wrong side, the broken-line effect that that creates on the right side will help with the blending. In fact, it doesn't. Make all your color changes on the right side of the rug.

COUNTING ROWS. When you need to count rows when knitting garter stitch, it's easier to count garter-stitch ridges (as indicated in the photo below). Each pair of garter-stitch rows makes one ridge. Use safety pins to mark every 5th or 10th garter-stitch ridge so you don't have to keep counting from the beginning. Slipping a marker made from contrasting fabric in between stitches is another good way to mark row counts.

IMPORTANT: In all of the patterns that follow, the first garter-stitch ridge in a new piece is created by the cast on and the knit-back row. The last garter-stitch ridge is created by the last row knitted on the right side, followed by the bind off.

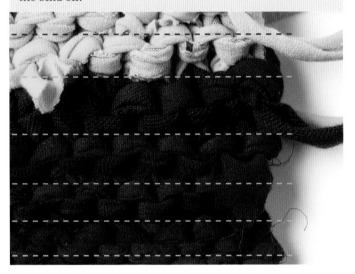

Starting a New Strip and Knitting On

Once you begin knitting, here's how to handle knots.

ENCOUNTERING KNOTS WITHOUT CHANGING COLOR. Whenever you see a knot coming up, tighten it as firmly as you can without tearing the fabric. Align one tail with the strip you're knitting with and knit the tail along with it as you approach the knot. Knit the knot, then knit the other tail in as you continue.

new tail

old tail and new working yarn

When you encounter a knot in the fabric strip, tighten it firmly, then hold one tail along with the working strip so that you can knit the two strips together as one. After you pass the knot, follow the same procedure with the other tail.

CHANGING COLORS AT THE END OF A ROW. When you have a bold color change at the end of the row, untie the strip at the nearest knot; cut the strip, leaving a long tail to use for stitching pieces together later; and twist the new yarn together with the old. Knit in the tail of the new color as you begin the next right-side row (for illustration of knitting in, see photo on the facing page. I recommend "knitting in" rather than catching the end behind your work, because a truly knit-in end won't show, whereas a carried-along end will dependably show up sooner or later. The dangling end is useful for sewing up, so be generous and make the tail 12 to 24 inches long. This way, you'll always have some sewing-up fiber in the right color, exactly where you need it, you won't have to attach a new length of fiber with backstitch, and the color will blend to be invisible.

CHANGING COLORS IN THE MIDDLE OF A ROW. Knot on a strip of the new color in the same way you knot like-colored strips together; then as you knit in the knot, align each tail with the section of working fiber that matches and knit it in.

APPROACHING THE END OF A ROW. To know whether you have enough fiber left to knit one more row, estimate that you will need three times the width of the row. Do not try to stretch a strip so that you can end a row with it if that leaves you with only an inch or so of fiber. It's better to shorten that strip, knot it somewhere in the middle of the row, and leave a generous tail.

Increase and Decrease Methods

This may be knitting heresy, but the truth is that it doesn't really matter what increase or decrease method you use when working with fabric strips: the increases and decreases don't show. I suggest knitting into the front and back for increases, and knitting 2 stitches together for decreases (see photos below). It's also not terribly important whether you make these increases or decreases in the first or last stitch of a row, or one stitch in from the edges. I usually make them right at the edges.

Increase: knit into front and back (kfb)

Decrease: knit 2 together (k2tog)

Binding Off

The bind off is always the second row in a pair of rows that creates a garter-stitch ridge. Always bind off on the wrong side of the fabric.

Bind off with the same tension you used when knitting the rest of the piece. A loose bind off will not show up against large-gauge garter stitch. A bind off that is too tight will create a narrower edge at the bound-off side, with the result that your units will not align correctly. In addition, your rug won't lie flat.

Just as when you're changing colors within a unit, when you bind off, leave 12- to 24-inch tails at the edges of each section to make the sewing up go easier. Allow a length of fiber about four times the length of a row for the bind off, in addition to the extra you need for the tail.

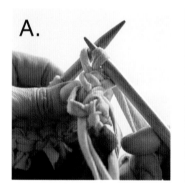 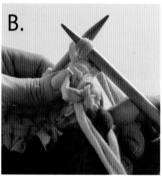

When binding off, leave long tails that you can later use for sewing pieces together. To bind off, knit 1 stitch (A), then knit the next stitch, and draw the first stitch over it and off the needle (B).

Assembling the Rug

Before sewing anything together, knit all the pieces. Last-minute design issues may appear when the modules are laid out on the table or floor, and it's much easier to change a layout that may have looked better on paper *before* you sew any of it together. If you are buying new fiber in a preplanned colorway, you may find this to be less of an issue than if you're working with randomly shaded, recycled fibers.

When I knit the first Teal Squares (page 111), I wanted each of the large blue squares to be one of four different shades. Perhaps fortunately, I accidentally knit 25 units, instead of the required 24, and had to swap the extra one in and out a few times to make my design work. You may be a more careful planner and not encounter this problem, or your color choices may not present a similar issue.

Lay the completed sections flat wherever you have enough space: on the floor, on a bed, or, if you're lucky, on a worktable. Once you find a layout that works, pin the pieces together with quilters' safety pins, carefully aligning garter-stitch ridges. I recommend pinning two pieces together, then setting that unit aside and pinning all similar pairs together. I then stitch all the pairs together before pinning the next level of modules. I don't want to have two seams on the same module pinned before sewing. In home economics sewing class, I learned not to cross seams without pressing. When you work with fabric strips, you aren't pressing seams, but the principle of having the seam neatly and securely made before moving to the next level applies just as much to seaming knit pieces as to seaming fabric.

I used to pin many modules together before doing any sewing, thinking I was being efficient, but that never gave great results, and it often meant I had to undo seams. Unpicking rag rug knitting is very hard because it's difficult to tell your stitching from the knitting. And if you accidentally cut a fabric strip that's been knit, rather than one that you used to sew the piece together, a hole shows up very quickly at 2 stitches to the inch.

Don't skimp on pins. Be generous with both the number and quality of the pins you use. I like to place them about 3 inches apart, and I've found that only strong pins work. Even if these are more expensive, they're worth it: the cheaper ones bend too much to be fun to use.

When I'm ready to sew, I thread the largest darning needle I can find with the same fiber I used for knitting the piece. Strips made from knits work better for stitching pieces together than those from woven fabric. Also, avoid using strips with seams for joining, as they're likely to separate. To ensure that my hand-stitched seams are secure, I backstitch at the start and end of each one.

I use a modified mattress stitch to join strips. If the join needs a bit more support, particularly if the edge-stitch fiber is a little flimsy, I take more than one stitch. (See photos below.)

Other tips for more successful assembly:

- Stitch along straight lines as long as possible by assembling small modules into stripes, rather than squares.
- Avoid pinning and sewing right-angle seams.
- Label the assembled strips by number, so that you can assemble them into the next-larger unit after all the first units are sewed up. This makes it less likely that you'll have to unpick a seam because you can't make it work, only to discover that something else was sewn in the wrong place and is causing the problem.

Using large, strong quilter's safety pins, place pins close together, perpendicular to the seam.

Stitch through at least one stitch from the bottom to the top of the fabric.

Move to the matching row on the other edge, and again sew through one stitch from the bottom to the top.

Borders . . . or Not?

Some of my rugs have borders, and some don't. One consideration is, "How clean are the edges?" If the stripes are strong and unified, they don't need an additional border. If the edge of the rug is a jumble, however, a border helps to contain the chaos and direct the viewer's attention back into the center of the rug, the way a frame does for other kinds of art. I take several different approaches to borders.

BORDERS KNIT IN STRIPS. One simple method is to knit 4-stitch-wide, one-color (usually black) strips. For this type border on square and rectangular rugs, count rows and match row and/or garter-stitch ridge counts to get the right fit. Attach the long sides of these borders first, making them the same length as the edges of the rug. Then attach the short sides so that they span the entire width, including the two lengthwise borders already applied.

Instead of knitting a solid-color border, you can knit the strips in color blocks that coordinate with the color of the rug. (Remember always to change colors on the right side of the strip.) As with solid-color borders, make these strips 4 stitches wide, one strip for each side of the rug. Disguise the fact that the border is attached in four sections by arranging your color selections so that the four corner blocks are black.

This border is one long strip, 4 stitches wide.

PIECED BORDERS. A completely different approach is to knit rectangular units of 8 to 12 stitches each. If you knit these units in different colors, the rug appears to be surrounded by concentric rectangles when stitched together and attached to the rug. (See, for example, the border around the Green and Peach Diagonal rug (page 64), which was "knit to fit.") This type of border features mitered corners. I recommend knitting the eight mitered corner units first, so that you can then adjust the sizes of the other border pieces to fit after you attach the corners.

To begin a mitered section, cast on a comfortable number of stitches, less four (that is, if you can easily work with 12 stitches on your needles, cast on 8). Knit in the color pattern, increasing 1 stitch at the corner end of the unit. *Note:* To ensure that the mitered corner units fit together correctly, you must make all increases on the right side and along the same edge of the piece. Do not increase on both the right and return rows of the same garter-stitch ridge. Make the increases on four of the border units along the left edge and four of them along the right edge. Note that these

This border was worked in modules using the same colors as were used in the main body of the rug.

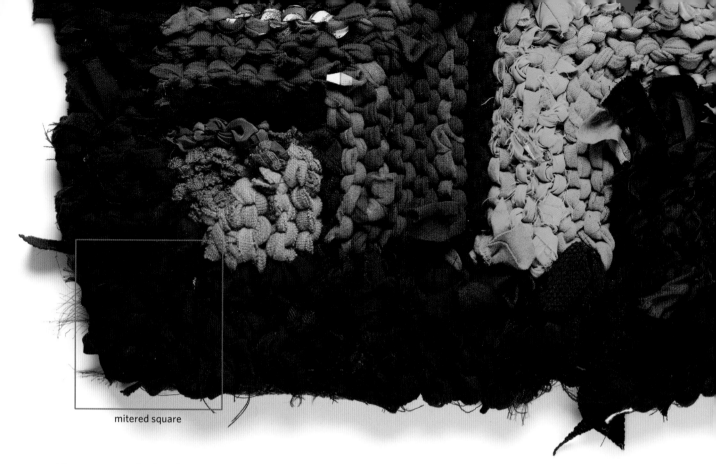

mitered square

This is an example of a border with mitered corners.

pieces are not reversible. Pin the corner units to the rug, but don't sew them to the rug yet. For an example of mitered corner units, see the instructions and charts on pages 133–34. (Reknit as many as you need to when you discover you got the miter on the wrong edge of the piece. It happens!)

To knit the rectangular units, first measure the distance between the corner pieces at the top, bottom, and sides. Divide each measurement into evenly spaced units equal to the largest number of stitches you can comfortably hold on your preferred needles. The size of the units at the top and bottom and at the sides does not have to be the same. For example, you may need three

12-stitch units to fill in along the top and bottom edges, while it might work out better to knit five 11-stitch units for the sides. No one will notice the difference.

Once you have knit all the pieces you need to fill in one side of the rug, you may choose to stop and pin them together and then to the rug, before finally stitching them to the rug. Or you can wait until you have all the pieces done. Expect some amount of unraveling, and even possibly sitting on the floor with your nearly finished rug to fit the last border unit in, stitch by stitch.

Borders for Circular Rugs

Take a different approach for a border on a round or irregularly shaped rug (such as spirals, triple spirals, or nautilus shapes). To get a good measurement for these borders, I borrowed a trick from woodworkers, who use a tool they call a "story stick" to get their measurements. Because of the way I use it, I call it a story strip.

Lay a piece of woven fabric along the outer edge of the rug all the way around, and mark on the woven fabric exactly the length of the piece you need to get to the desired length. It's important that the story strip be made of woven fabric; knitted fabric will stretch, so that the measurement becomes distorted.

To knit the border, cast on 3 stitches, and check your progress against your story strip by pinning your knitting to it every foot or so. You may need to throw in an occasional short row to encourage the strip to curve around the rug and lie flat; short rows aren't needed if you make your border only 2 stitches wide. You'll see your progress as you knit.

Sometimes, You Just Have to Make It Up!

Having given you all this information that will help you make beautiful fabric rugs and have a lot of fun doing so, there's one more piece of advice: Sometimes you have to muck around a bit to make things come out right. Even though I design rugs on graph paper, then knit from my plan, sometimes adjustments must be made along the way.

You'll benefit from some of the things I've learned from experience, such as how and when to work short rows in spiral rugs, for example, but I hope, too, that you'll explore different ways of doing things that work better for you.

You'll also learn by carrying out your own experiments. For instance, you might decide on a certain color for the border, but rather than knitting the whole border and deciding you don't like it, knit a swatch. At 2 stitches to an inch, it doesn't take long at all to knit up a test square for a border to see how the colors you're thinking of using look against the completed rug. If you don't like them, start over. Make another decision.

If you hate a certain knitting technique, for heaven's sake, don't use it. For instance, I tried the traditional pick-up-and-knit technique when I first began to work with log cabin designs, and it drove me nuts — far too much picking up for my taste. Allowing myself to try a different approach cleared the way to develop the diagonally striped patterns that create much the same effect in much less time and infinitely less aggravation. Allow yourself to discover your own solutions!

CHAPTER 4

Earn Your Stripes

The striped rugs in this chapter are all worked in simple back-and-forth garter-stitch rows, with sections extending the full width or length of the rug.

For one of the very first striped rugs, I cast on 10 to 14 stitches and knit in garter stitch until I had the length I wanted. I worked the colors randomly, paying no particular attention to whether they changed on the front or back. I knit several strips in the same manner, bound off, then assembled the strips. I had to knit some extra bits to make it all work out. Casual knitting like this is fine as far as it goes. If you want more formality and control over the outcome, however, you need to do more planning up front.

01 / Tweedy Red Stripes

You can do some amazing things with basic stripes when you plan color changes and control the number of rows. I knit this rug, Tweedy Stripes, in reds because the red stash was overflowing and I needed to reduce the volume. The strong reds of medium value used in Stripes #3 and #5 (see page 53) are an especially easy-to-collect shade of red. Because I wanted to use as much red as possible, I tied in tiny bits of accent colors, rather than blocks or stripes that would use a color other than red. The accent colors are similar in value to the stripe I knit them into. (For value, see page 32.) Each individual strip of accent color ranges from 12" to 20" long, to create variety in the size of the tweedy bits.

For the rug shown, I had the least amount of fabric for the shade of red I used for Stripe #2, but what I had was sufficiently different from either of its neighbors that I wanted to make a separate stripe. Note that because of the anticipated shortage, this stripe has one less stitch in the cast on.

The stripes run widthwise, because I wanted them to be wide enough that they were fun to knit. I don't like turning the needles all the time, and stripes that are six stitches or fewer turn too often. An even number of stripes puts a seam right down the middle, whereas with five, there's a nice stripe down the middle — much more visually pleasing, so this rug has five, not six. I shaded the colors from one side to the other, moving from dark at the edge to lighter toward the middle, and then becoming darker at the other edge.

Because I knit to length rather than to a row count, the sections in the middle are a little too short. (The outside stripes have

34 garter-stitch ridges, while the inside stripes have only 32.) For a neater edge, instead of "knitting to fit," count garter-stitch ridges so that all strips match more accurately in length. Laying pieces on top of each other to check length, particularly when one of the sections is still on the needle, does not give an accurate result. The directions below suggest counting garter-stitch ridges instead, so that your sections are the same length.

(See Changing Colors and Counting Garter-Stitch Rows, page 40.)

Project Overview

- The fabrics used for this rug are predominantly a range of reds, with shades of pink, orange, yellow, blue, aqua, violet, and green (optional, to taste) as accents.

- Make each stripe 32 garter-stitch ridges long.

- The cast on is the first row of the first garter-stitch ridge; the bind off is the second row of the last garter-stitch ridge.

- Leave 12- to 20-inch-long tails at both the cast on and the bind off, as well as each time you start a new strip.

FINISHED MEASUREMENTS
31" wide × 24" long

Knitting Tweedy Red Stripes

Knit 5 stripes using the colors and containing the number of stitches indicated in the table below. Each stripe should be 32 garter-stitch ridges long.

STRIPE #	NUMBER OF STITCHES	COLOR
1	8	Darkest reds
2	7	Dark reds
3	14	Strong, medium-value reds
4	11	Lightest reds
5	14	Strong, medium-value reds

- Darkest reds
- Dark reds
- Medium reds
- Lightest reds

| STRIPE 1 | STRIPE 2 | STRIPE 3 | STRIPE 4 | STRIPE 5 |

RUG ASSEMBLY

Pin two strips together aligning garter-stitch ridges. Join, using a modified mattress stitch (see page 43). Repeat until all the strips have been joined together.

32 garter-stitch ridges

| 8 sts | 7 sts | 14 sts | 11 sts | 14 sts |

Design Theories from the Math World

You can achieve a number of different effects by playing with the proportions of your stripes. Working stripes of different widths can make a rug more interesting. Experiment with colored pencils or fabric swatches on a test paper pattern to figure out what stripe width works best for you. At the same time, changes in color can produce the optical illusion of different widths, too, so a narrower stripe of a brighter color may look exactly as wide as a wider stripe of a duller color.

Mathematical guidelines can also help you make your rug look good. For instance, the Rule of Thirds, the Golden Mean, and the Fibonacci sequence can all provide good templates for your work. (From another point of view, the principle behind each of these gives pretty much the same result.) The more rugs you make, the easier it will be to incorporate these guidelines into your design at the paper stages.

GOLDEN MEAN. You can use the principle of the Golden Mean (or Golden Ratio) to determine pleasing dimensions for a rectangular rug. Draw a square, then extend one side to make a rectangle that measures the length of the original square multiplied by 1.62. Rectangles with these proportions have "looked good" since the Greeks built the Parthenon.

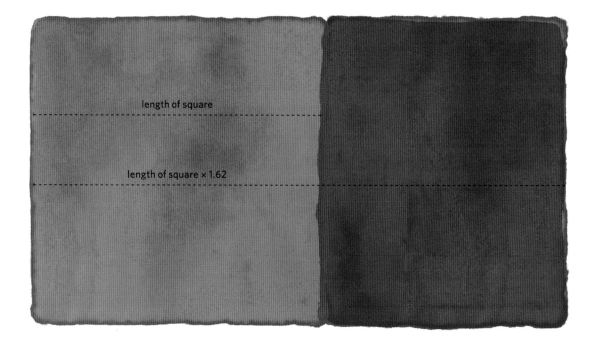

length of square

length of square × 1.62

FIBONACCI SEQUENCE. In the Fibonacci sequence, each number is the sum of the two previous numbers: 1, 1, 2, 3, 5, 8, 13, and so on. Any two numbers (after 1) in the sequence can be used to determine the length and width of a rectangular rug; the finished proportions will be close to the Golden Mean.

In nature, spirals develop according to the Fibonacci sequence; that is, any one section of a spiral will be the size of the previous two sections added together. I have not used this principle in my own spiral rugs, because although it's easy to knit up to 8 or maybe 13 stitches on a needle, more than that is difficult to impossible.

THE RULE OF THIRDS. The Rule of Thirds states that pictures look better when the center of interest is *not* at the center of the picture, but rather at the intersection of lines breaking the space into thirds. Use the Rule of Thirds to decide where to place major color changes and to avoid placing a seam down the exact middle of a rug. In addition, this rule suggests that an odd number of stripes will always look better than an even number.

In nature, spirals develop according to the Fibonacci sequence. That is, any one section of a spiral will be the size of the previous two sections added together.

In this design, I avoided placing a seam down the center, one of the precepts of the rule of thirds.

02

Biltmore Floating Stripes

When you're planning a design that depends on a large background area of a fairly consistent hue, select commonly available colors. I had originally planned for Biltmore Stripes to be four times as big as it is, but as I worked through my stock of gold fabrics, I realized there wasn't going to be enough fiber. I cut down the paper pattern and used what I had. Compare my first sketches on page 61 to the finished rug, and you'll see that they aren't the same, except for one section. There is a visible seam down the middle of the pale yellow stripe, pretty nearly in the exact middle of this rug. Were I to knit it again, another change would be to knit seven vertical units to avoid having a seam in the exact center of the rug.

This design requires a clear demarcation between foreground and background. For color inspiration, I used paint chips from the hardware store. It would be interesting to try a reverse color scheme, with the darks as the background. It's hard, however, to find a large enough quantity of strong purple and royal blue in the recycle stream.

Project Overview

- This rug consists of six vertical stripes: two gold, two pale yellow, one very light green, and one a more olive-green. The horizontal bars are brown, dark green, royal blue, and purple. Because it's important that the bars align when you assemble this rug, be sure to very carefully count garter-stitch ridges. You also have to make sure to change colors on the right side only; the broken lines of reverse garter-stitch ridges are horribly apparent, and you'll only have to rip those rows out if you make a mistake.

- Knit each stripe following the stitch and garter-stitch ridge counts in the color progression chart (facing page) and the watercolor plan and graphed charts (page 60).

- For every stripe, the cast on is the first row of the first garter-stitch ridge, and the second row of the last garter-stitch ridge is the bind off.

FINISHED MEASUREMENTS
38" wide × 31" long

- Gold
- Brown
- Dark green
- Royal blue
- Purple
- Light yellow
- Light green
- Olive green

Knitting Biltmore Floating Stripes

Knit 6 stripes using the color progressions and containing the number of stitches indicated in the table below. Each stripe should be 48 garter-stitch ridges long. Colors are listed in the order knit (the first horizontal gold bar will be at the bottom of the stripe).

STRIPE #1 (12 STITCHES)

COLOR	GARTER-STITCH RIDGE COUNT
Gold	6
Brown	4
Gold	4
Dark green	4
Gold	4
Royal blue	4
Gold	12
Brown	4
Gold	6

STRIPE #2 (12 STITCHES)

COLOR	GARTER-STITCH RIDGE COUNT
Gold	6
Brown	4
Gold	4
Dark green	4
Gold	12
Purple	4
Gold	4
Brown	4
Gold	6

STRIPE #3 (8 STITCHES)

COLOR	GARTER-STITCH RIDGE COUNT
Light yellow	14
Dark green	4
Light yellow	4
Brown	4
Light yellow	4
Purple	4
Light yellow	14

STRIPE #4 (7 STITCHES)

COLOR	GARTER-STITCH RIDGE COUNT
Light yellow	6
Purple	4
Light yellow	12
Brown	4
Light yellow	4
Purple	4
Light yellow	4
Royal blue	4
Light yellow	6

STRIPE #5 (12 STITCHES)

COLOR	GARTER-STITCH RIDGE COUNT
Light green	6
Purple	4
Light green	4
Royal blue	4
Light green	4
Brown	4
Light green	12
Royal blue	4
Light green	6

STRIPE #6 (12 STITCHES)

COLOR	GARTER-STITCH RIDGE COUNT
Olive green	6
Purple	4
Olive green	4
Royal blue	4
Olive green	12
Dark green	4
Olive green	4
Royal blue	4
Olive green	6

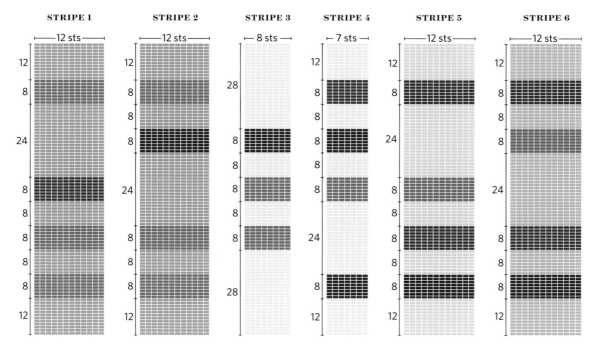

STRIPE 1	STRIPE 2	STRIPE 3	STRIPE 4	STRIPE 5	STRIPE 6
12 sts	12 sts	8 sts	7 sts	12 sts	12 sts

*Note: This chart shows **row** counts, not garter-stitch rows.*

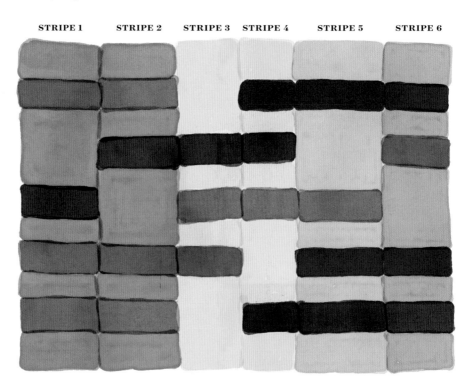

RUG ASSEMBLY

Use safety pins to fasten all the stripes together, taking care to align the garter-stitch ridges and the color bars so that they appear to "float" across the stripes. See page 43 for information on how to sew the pieces together.

Check for a pleasing arrangement of the bars. Work your plan for a rug like Biltmore Stripes on graph paper with colored pencils. Be sure to look at it from a distance, squinting, and in bad light. Look for "rivers," where your eye unintentionally follows blank space through the rug. Check the vertical alignment of the ends of the floating bars so that you're not creating unplanned elements. Notice that none of the ends of the floating bars aligns with another, unless there are solid bars in between. The color transition between the different background stripes is where the vertical element of this rug appears.

Consider creating a mock-up. If you're someone who can't bear to find mistakes or face do-overs in your finished knitting, draw out your design full size before you knit. You'll see your design differently at this scale. You might want to move the color bars around the rug, and this is easier to do on paper than on the actual finished rug.

03 / Green and Peach Diagonal Stripes

Once you've mastered knitting a rug consisting of straight stripes, try one with diagonals. In order to create the diagonal, decrease at the start of every right-side row and increase at the start of the next wrong-side row. (To create a diagonal that slants in the opposite direction, increase at the start of right-side rows and decrease at the start of the next wrong-side row.) Knitting stripes on the diagonal is speed-demon knitting. Changing colors on the whole row is a no-brainer. And the patterns that can be developed with careful color management are magnificent.

Project Overview

- The first stripe in this six-stripe pattern is an ordered set of color blocks, knit in alternating dark-neutral and rosy-colored bands. (See Color Progression, page 65.)

- The color progression and number of garter-stitch ridges to be knit with each color is the same for each stripe (except for the "eyes"), no matter what the stitch count is. However, the point at which you start the color progression varies from stripe to stripe and is specified in the instructions. It's important to count the rows carefully to ensure that the bands of each color line up at the edges to create chevrons.

- Two focal points — "eyes" — are created by knitting a small triangle that interrupts the diagonals. The long edges (hypotenuses) of the triangles on adjacent stripes abut to form a diamond-shaped eye. The diagonals above the eye run in the opposite direction of those below.

- To begin each stripe, place a slip knot on your left-hand needle, then knit into the back of it to cast on one more stitch. Knit these 2 stitches. This is the first garter-stitch ridge.

- To end each stripe, work until 2 stitches remain, knit these 2 stitches, then k2tog to bind off. This is the last garter-stitch ridge.

- Leave 12- to 20-inch-long tails at both the cast on and the bind off, as well as each time you start a new strip.

- The border, which has mitered corners, is knit in blocks of 14 stitches in black, brown, maroon, and dark green.

ABBREVIATIONS

kfb — Knit into the front and then into the back of a stitch before slipping from the needle

k2tog — Knit 2 stitches together

eyes

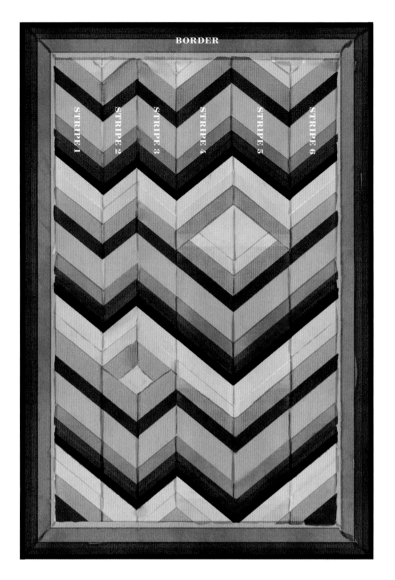

BORDER

STRIPE 1 STRIPE 2 STRIPE 3 STRIPE 4 STRIPE 5 STRIPE 6

- Brown
- Dark peach
- Light green
- Light pink
- Black
- Maroon
- Dark green
- Medium green

Color Progression

(Note: This is an 18-ridge repeat.)

COLOR	GARTER-STITCH RIDGES
Brown	2
Dark peach	3
Light green (olive overtones)	2
Light pink	2
Black	1
Brown	1
Maroon	1
Dark green	2
Medium green (blue overtones)	4

Border Color Progression

COLOR	GARTER-STITCH RIDGES
Medium green	1
Dark green	2
Maroon	1
Brown	1
Black	2

FINISHED MEASUREMENTS

40" wide × 59" long

STRIPE #1

The diagonals on this stripe slant from lower right to upper left. There are three and a half repeats of this sequence up this stripe, beginning with Brown.

Setup. Using brown, place a slip knot on your left-hand needle, then knit into the back of it to cast on one more stitch. Knit these 2 stitches. (1 garter-stitch ridge)

INCREASE ROWS

Following the color progression and garter-stitch ridge counts (page 65), kfb at the beginning of **each row**, and work until you have 12 stitches. (6 brown garter-stitch ridges total)

KNITTING THE DIAGONALS

Repeat the following 2 rows, continuing the color progression, until you have 57 garter-stitch ridges and are ready to start the second of 3 dark peach ridges. The stitch count remains constant at 12, and you are creating a stripe with a diagonal that slants from lower right to upper left.

Right-side rows. K2tog, knit to end.

Wrong-side rows. Kfb, knit to end.

DECREASE ROWS

Continuing to follow the color progression, k2tog at the beginning of **each row** until you have 1 stitch.

Cut the fabric strip, leaving a 12- to 20-inch tail, and draw the tail through the last stitch to fasten off.

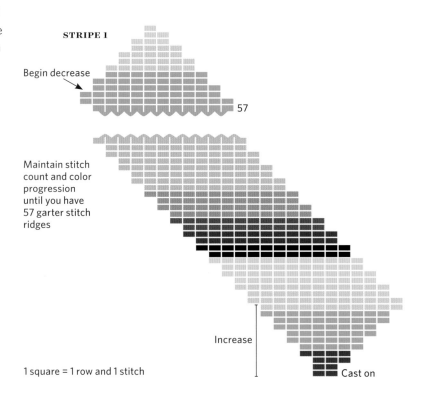

STRIPE 1

Begin decrease

57

Maintain stitch count and color progression until you have 57 garter stitch ridges

Increase

Cast on

1 square = 1 row and 1 stitch

STRIPE #2 (includes first half of the small eye)

The diagonals on this stripe slant from lower right to upper left at the start, then slant in the opposite direction above the eye. The stripe begins with light green.

Setup. Using light green, place a slip knot on your left-hand needle, then knit into the back of it to cast on one more stitch. Knit these 2 stitches. (1 garter-stitch ridge)

INCREASE ROWS
Following the color progression, kfb at the beginning of **each row**, and work until you have 7 stitches. (4 light green garter-stitch ridges total)

KNITTING THE DIAGONALS
Repeat the following 2 rows, continuing the color progression, until you have 15 garter-stitch ridges and are ready to knit with dark peach. The stitch count remains constant at 7.

Right-side rows. K2tog, knit to end.

Wrong-side rows. Kfb, to end.

WORKING THE EYE
Using dark peach, repeat the following 2 rows, until you have 4 stitches. (3 dark peach ridges)

Right-side rows. K2tog, knit to end.

Wrong-side rows. Work even.

Change to light green. Repeat the following 2 rows until you have 1 stitch. (3 light green ridges)

Right-side rows. K2tog, knit to end.

Wrong-side rows. Work even.

Pickup. With the one remaining stitch still on the needles and the right side facing you, use dark peach to pick up 6 stitches along the left edge of the stripe, turn, and knit back. (7 stitches)

Next row (wrong side). K2tog, knit to end. (1 dark peach ridge)

COMPLETING STRIPE #2
Repeat the following 2 rows, continuing the color progression, until you have 40 garter-stitch ridges from where you picked up with dark peach. The diagonals above the eye now slant from lower left to upper right.

(continued on next page)

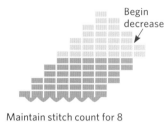

Begin decrease

Maintain stitch count for 8 color progressions

STRIPE 2

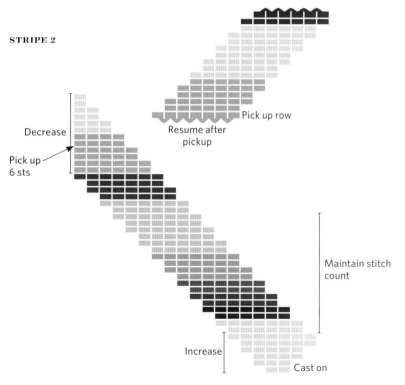

Decrease

Pick up 6 sts

Pick up row

Resume after pickup

Maintain stitch count

Increase

Cast on

Right-side rows. Kfb, knit to end (7 stitches).

Wrong-side rows. K2tog, knit to end.

DECREASE ROWS
Starting with the second of 2 light green ridges and following the color progression, k2tog at the beginning of **each row** until you have 1 stitch.

Cut the fabric strip, leaving a 12- to 20-inch tail, and draw the tail through the last stitch to fasten off.

STRIPE #3 (includes second half of the small eye)

The diagonals on this stripe slant from lower left to upper right at the start, then slant in the opposite direction above the eye. The stripe begins with light green.

Setup. Using light green, place a slip knot on your left-hand needle, then knit into the back of it to cast on one more stitch. Turn and knit these 2 stitches. (1 garter-stitch ridge)

INCREASE ROWS
Following the color progression, kfb at the beginning of **each row**, and work until you have 7 stitches. (3 light green garter-stitch ridges total)

KNITTING THE DIAGONALS
Repeat the following 2 rows, continuing the color progression, until you have 15 garter-stitch ridges and are ready to knit with dark peach. The stitch count remains constant at 7 stitches.

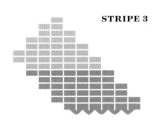

STRIPE 3

Right-side rows. Kfb, knit to end.

Wrong-side rows. K2tog, to end.

WORKING THE EYE
Using dark peach, repeat the following 2 rows until you have 4 stitches (3 dark peach ridges).

Right-side rows. Knit to end of row.

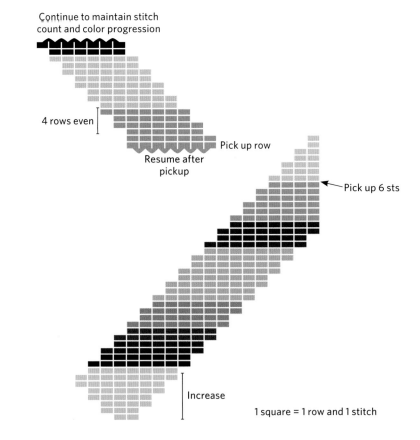

Continue to maintain stitch count and color progression

4 rows even

Resume after pickup

Pick up row

Pick up 6 sts

Increase

1 square = 1 row and 1 stitch

Wrong-side rows. K2tog, knit to end of row.

Change to light green. Repeat the following 2 rows until you have 1 stitch. (3 light green ridges)

Right-side rows. Knit to end of row.

Wrong-side rows. K2tog, knit to end of row.

Pickup. With the remaining stitch on the needle and the wrong side facing you, use dark peach to pick up 6 stitches along the right edge of the stripe. The pickup row forms the first dark peach ridge. (7 stitches)

Next row (right side). K2tog, knit to end.

Next row (wrong side). Kfb, knit to end.

COMPLETING STRIPE #3
Repeat the following 2 rows, continuing the color progression, until you have 40 garter-stitch ridges from where you picked up with dark peach. The diagonals above the eye slant from lower right to upper left.

Right-side rows. K2tog, knit to end.

Wrong-side rows. Kfb, knit to end. (7 stitches)

DECREASE ROWS
Starting with the second of 2 light green ridges and following the color progression, k2tog at the beginning of **each row** until you have 1 stitch.

Cut the fabric strip, leaving a 12- to 20-inch tail, and draw the tail through the last stitch to fasten off.

STRIPE #4 (includes first half of the large eye)

The diagonals on this stripe slant from lower right to upper left at the start, then slant in the opposite direction above the break. The stripe begins with light green.

Setup. Using light green, place a slip knot on your left-hand needle, then knit into the back of it to cast on one more stitch. Knit these 2 stitches. (1 garter-stitch ridge)

INCREASE ROWS
Following the color progression, kfb at the beginning of **each row**, and work until you have 14 stitches. (7 light green garter-stitch ridges total)

KNITTING THE DIAGONALS
Repeat the following 2 rows, continuing the color progression, until you have 34 garter-stitch ridges and are ready to knit the second garter-stitch ridge of dark peach.

Right-side rows. K2tog, knit to end.

Wrong-side rows. Kfb, knit to end. (14 stitches)

WORKING THE EYE
Note: You do not follow the color progression as established to work this eye.

Next row (right side). Using dark peach, k2tog, knit to end.

Next row (wrong side). Work even.

Repeat these 2 rows until you have 12 stitches. (3 dark peach garter-stitch ridges)

Change to light green.

Next row. K2tog, knit to end.

Next row. Work even.

Repeat these 2 rows until you have 9 stitches. (3 light green garter-stitch ridges)

Change to light peach.

Next row. K2tog, knit to end.

Next row. Work even.

Repeat these 2 rows until 1 stitch remains.

Pickup. With the remaining stitch on the needle and the right side facing you, use dark peach to pick up 13 stitches along the left edge of the stripe, turn, and knit back. (14 stitches)

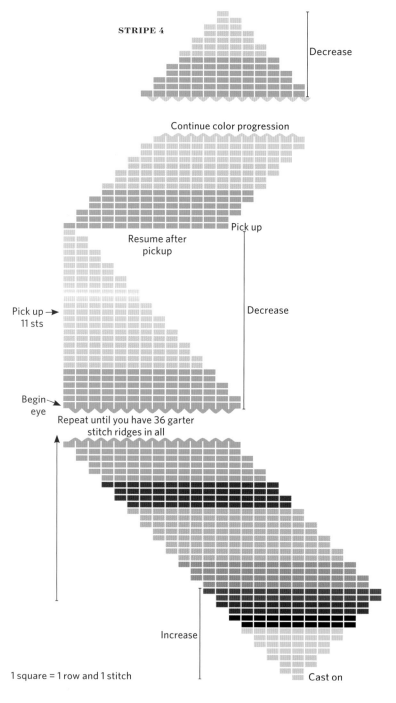

STRIPE 4

Decrease

Continue color progression

Pick up

Resume after pickup

Pick up →
11 sts

Decrease

Begin →
eye

Repeat until you have 36 garter stitch ridges in all

Increase

1 square = 1 row and 1 stitch

Cast on

Next row (wrong side). K2tog, knit to end.

Next row (right side). Kfb, knit to end.

Repeat these 2 rows until there are 3 dark peach garter-stitch ridges, including pickup row, ending with a wrong-side row.

COMPLETING STRIPE #4

Repeat the following 2 rows, again continuing the color progression, until you have 18 garter-stitch ridges from where you picked up with dark peach. The diagonals above the eye slant from lower left to upper right.

Right-side rows. Kfb, knit to end. (14 stitches)

Wrong-side rows. K2tog, knit to end.

DECREASE ROWS

Following the color progression, k2tog at the beginning of **each row** until you have 1 stitch.

Cut the fabric strip, leaving a 12- to 20-inch tail, and draw the tail through the last stitch to fasten off.

STRIPE #5 (includes second half of the large eye)

The diagonals on this stripe slant from lower left to upper right, then slant in the opposite direction above the break. The stripe begins with light green.

Setup. Using light green, place a slip knot on your left-hand needle, then knit into the back of it to cast on one more stitch. Knit these 2 stitches. (1 garter-stitch ridge)

INCREASE ROWS
Following the color progression, kfb at the beginning of **each row**, and work until you have 13 stitches. (6 garter-stitch ridges total)

KNITTING THE DIAGONALS
Repeat the following 2 rows, continuing the color progression, until you have 34 garter-stitch ridges and are ready to knit the second garter-stitch ridge in dark peach.

Right-side rows. Kfb, knit to end. (14 stitches)

Wrong-side rows. K2tog, to end.

WORKING THE EYE
Note: You do not follow the color progression as established to work this eye.

Next row (right side). Using dark peach, knit to end.

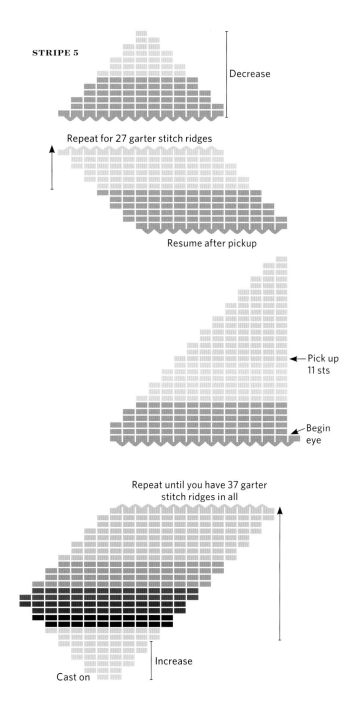

STRIPE 5

Decrease

Repeat for 27 garter stitch ridges

Resume after pickup

← Pick up 11 sts

← Begin eye

Repeat until you have 37 garter stitch ridges in all

Increase

Cast on

Next row (wrong side). K2tog, knit to end.

Repeat these 2 rows until you have 11 stitches. (3 dark peach garter-stitch ridges)

Change to light green.

Next row. Work even.

Next row. K2tog, knit to end.

Repeat these 2 rows until you have 8 stitches. (3 light green garter-stitch ridges)

Change to light peach.

Next row. Work even.

Next row. K2tog, knit to end.

Repeat these 2 rows until 1 stitch remains.

Pickup. With the remaining stitch on your needle and the wrong side facing you, use dark peach to pick up 13 stitches along the right edge of the stripe. The pickup row forms the first dark peach ridge. (14 stitches)

Next row (right side). K2tog, knit to end.

Next row (wrong side). Kfb, knit to end.

Repeat these 2 rows until there are 3 dark peach garter-stitch ridges, including the pickup row, ending with a wrong-side row.

COMPLETING STRIPE #5

Repeat the following 2 rows, continuing the color progression, until you have 18 garter-stitch ridges from where you picked up with dark peach. The diagonals above the break slant from lower right to upper left.

Right-side rows. K2tog, knit to end.

Wrong side rows. Kfb, knit to end. (14 stitches)

DECREASE ROWS

Following the color progression, k2tog at the beginning of **each row** until you have 1 stitch.

Cut the fabric strip, leaving a 12- to 20-inch tail, and draw the tail through the last stitch to fasten off.

STRIPE #6

The diagonals on this stripe slant from lower left to upper right. The stripe begins with brown.

Setup. Using brown, place a slip knot on your left-hand needle, then knit into the back of it to cast on one more stitch. Knit these 2 stitches. (1 garter-stitch ridge)

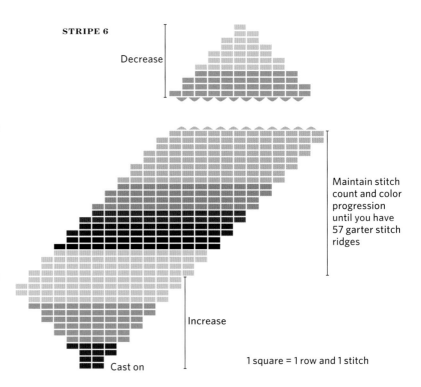

STRIPE 6

Decrease

Maintain stitch count and color progression until you have 57 garter stitch ridges

Increase

Cast on

1 square = 1 row and 1 stitch

INCREASE ROWS

Following the color progression, kfb at the beginning of **each row**, and work until you have 12 stitches. (6 garter-stitch ridges total)

KNITTING THE DIAGONALS

Repeat the following 2 rows, continuing the color progression, until you have 57 garter-stitch ridges. The stitch count remains at 12 stitches.

Right-side rows. Kfb, knit to end.

Wrong-side rows. K2tog, to end. (12 stitches)

DECREASE ROWS

Following the color progression, k2tog at the beginning of **each row** until you have 1 stitch.

Cut the fabric strip, leaving a 12- to 20-inch tail, and draw the tail through the last stitch to fasten off.

ASSEMBLING THE RUG

Assemble the rug before knitting the border pieces. Pin each stripe in order, taking care to match color bands and garter-stitch ridges, especially where the diagonal slants change to create the eyes. Use mattress stitch (see page 43) to sew the stripes together.

KNITTING AND ATTACHING BORDER

The border is knit in rectangular sections, and attached to the finished rug with the garter-stitch ridges parallel to the edge. Eight corner sections have increases along one edge so that when assembled with these diagonal edges abutting, they form miters for the corners. Most of the rectangular sections between the corner sections are 12 stitches in length, but you will need to knit some sections on each side "to fit."

Work the Corner Border Sections (see next page for color charts), then position them on the rug so that the diagonal edges abut to form miters. Pin them to the rug. Do not sew these pieces to the rug yet.

Measure the longest side of one of the corner pieces to determine your approximate gauge over 12 stitches. Then measure the spaces between the corner pieces on each of the four sides. Divide each of those measurements by your gauge. This gives you the number of Rectangular Border Sections you'll need to knit. You're unlikely to get an even number, so make one or more pieces shorter (or longer) as needed in order to fill the space.

Once you have knit all the pieces you need to fill the gap on one side of the rug, you may choose to stop and pin them together and to the rug, then stitch. Or you can wait until you have all the pieces done.

CORNER BORDER SECTION #1
(make 4)

Setup. Cast on 8 stitches in medium green, and knit back. (1 garter-stitch ridge)

Follow the color progression as you work the increase rows:

Right-side row. Knit to last stitch, kfb.

Wrong-side row. Work even.

Repeat these 2 rows until you have 13 stitches and have completed 3 rows of black.

Bind off in black. (The bind off forms the second row of the last garter-stitch ridge.)

CORNER BORDER SECTION #2
(make 4)

Setup. Cast on 8 stitches in medium green, and knit back. (1 garter-stitch ridge)

(continued on next page)

Follow the color progression as you work the increase rows:

Right-side row. Kfb, knit to end.

Wrong-side row. Work even.

Repeat these 2 rows until you have 13 stitches and have completed 3 rows of black.

Bind off in black. (The bind off forms the second row of the last garter-stitch ridge.)

RECTANGULAR BORDER SECTION

Make as many as necessary. You may need to make one on each side a few stitches longer or shorter than the directions below specify in order to get the correct length. As usual, the cast on is the first row of the first garter-stitch ridge and the bind off is the second row of the last garter-stitch ridge.

Setup. Cast on (about) 12 stitches in medium green, then knit back. Follow the table for the color progression and garter-stitch rib count.

CORNER BORDER SECTION #1

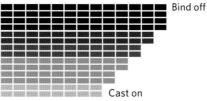

Bind off

Cast on

CORNER BORDER SECTION #2

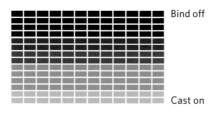

Bind off

Cast on

RECTANGULAR BORDER SECTION

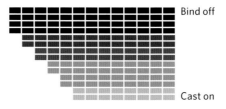

Bind off

Cast on

1 square = 1 row and 1 stitch

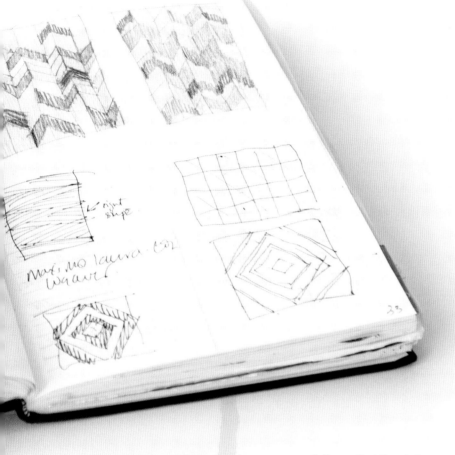

These stripes with diagonal stitch patterns are similar to the flamelike stitches characteristic of Bargello needlepoint embroidery. In an earlier version of the design (see drawing above), the diagonals in half the stripes run from lower left to upper right; in the other half, they run from upper left to lower right. In the assembled rug, the direction of the diagonals alternates from one to the other. It is important to count garter-stitch ridges carefully so that the stripes line up at the edges to create chevrons.

For Green and Peach Diagonals, I took the concept further and went "freestyle," adding "eyes" that serve as focal points in the design. I created these eyes by changing the direction of the diagonals at specific points on two pairs of adjacent stripes and carefully aligning them so that visually they appear to be squares.

These elaborate color changes are fun to work out on graph paper. Now that it is completed, looking at this rug makes me want to caution you not to get too carried away. In a Bargello-like pattern such as this, you're working with two different design elements: color shading and the interplay of light and dark. I would like to have had three complete peach bands and four green, but that would have made the rug at least 25 percent bigger in both dimensions; which is a 56 percent increase in area (and, therefore, weight). I could have knit fewer repetitions of each color, but then the horizontal bands of color would have been thinner (fewer garter-stitch ridges each), which might not look as good.

This confirms my advice always to test — and be willing to knit again. When in doubt, knit the rug that comes out smaller first. If you don't like it, you'll find out in a shorter amount of time.

04

Floating Gold Square

An art quilt gave me the idea for the Floating Squares series: "float" an area of a different color over a base of shaded stripes. I already had a system for creating a graduated blend of colors along the length of a stripe (see Developing Blending Patterns, page 81). Adding a "float" over the stripes was a new challenge. How could that work? I played around with the concept and realized it could be done. It will be interesting to float a curved shape over a similar base, but to date, that design has eluded me. Floating Gold Square is my first successful rug in this series.

At first glance, this rug appears to be composed of three shaded stripes, but in fact, it has seven vertical stripes. The outer two stripes are #1 and #7. Just in from these are stripes in which gold interrupts the gradual shading at their centers (#2 and #6). These form the edges of the large gold square in the center. The middle three stripes (#3, #4, and #5) have the same color patterning as the ones next to them, but the middle three reverse the progression of the shading, so that the darkest and lightest sections fall at the opposite ends, keeping the yellow square in the center constant.

To make the block in the center "float," one garter-stitch ridge of the floated color replaces one of the garter-stitch ridges of the base color. The floating color itself is slightly shaded, with more greenish-golds at the bottom and yellower golds at the top. (This shading can be seen more clearly in the photo of the black, white, and red floating square rug on page 81.)

Project Overview

- In Floating Gold Square, the darkest color is a purple (AAAA) that is almost black. The color progression moves from there through a medium purple to beige to almost white (HHHH).

- Following the color progression and stitch counts for each stripe (see tables on opposite page), work 4 garter-stitch ridges in each of the color blends. Each unit has 60 garter-stitch ridges.

- For every stripe, the cast on is the first row of the first garter-stitch ridge, and the second-row of the last garter-stitch ridge is the bind off.

- If you want the rug a bit smaller, knit fewer rows of the solid color blocks — for example, either 2 (AA) or 3 (AAA) garter-stitch ridges. However, you need at least 4 ridges to make the smooth color change between solid blocks (ABAB).

FINISHED MEASUREMENTS
33" wide × 42" long

Stitch Counts

STRIPE #	STITCH COUNT
1	12
2	8
3	5
4	5
5	5
6	8
7	12

Knitting the Floating Squares Rug

Knit 7 stripes, following the tables below for stitch counts and color progressions. Work 1 garter-stitch ridge of each color in a blend set (4 garter-stitch ridges for each blend). For example, for AAAA of Stripe #1 of Floating Gold Square, knit 4 garter stitch ridges (8 rows) of the lightest color. For BABA, work 1 ridge of B, 1 ridge of A, 1 of B, and 1 of A: 4 garter-stitch ridges in all (8 rows). Note that gold is specified by color, instead of by letter, as it is not part of the shade blend (see Project Overview). Each stripe consists of 60 garter-stitch ridges.

STRIPES #1 AND #7 (12 STITCHES WIDE)	STRIPES #2 AND #6 (8 STITCHES WIDE)	STRIPES #3, #4, AND #5 (5 STITCHES WIDE)
AAAA	AAAA	HHHH
BABA	BABA	HGHG
BBBB	BBBB	GFGF
CBCB	C-gold-C-gold	F-gold-F-gold
CCCC	C-gold-C-gold	F-gold-E-gold
DCDC	C-gold-D-gold	E-gold-E-gold
DDDD	D-gold-D-gold	E-gold-D-gold
EDED	D-gold-E-gold	D-gold-D-gold
EEEE	E-gold-E-gold	D-gold-C-gold
FEFE	E-gold-F-gold	C-gold-C-gold
FFFF	F-gold-F-gold	C-gold-C-gold
GFGF	GFGF	BCBC
GGGG	GGGG	BBBB
HGHG	HGHG	ABAB
HHHH	HHHH	AAAA

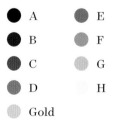

● A   ● E
● B   ● F
● C   ● G
● D   ○ H
● Gold

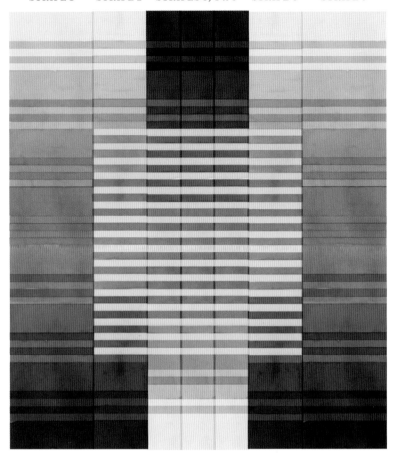

FLOATING SQUARE ASSEMBLY

Sew the stripes together by aligning garter-stitch ridges, being extra careful to align the colors in the floating box. Any misalignment will jump out at you if you get this wrong. Also, if you mount the rug on a backing, it's important to make sure you attach the floating color in a straight line.

Developing Blending Patterns

One day when I was playing with my stash, I thought of Ansel Adams and his Zone System, which many photographers use to determine the correct exposure for photographs. I realized that this system could be adapted to categorize colors for a rug from darkest to lightest.

Begin by sorting your colors by shade, darkest to lightest, with no gaps. Make sure to sort the colors in daylight without a filter of any kind, then check your work with red lenses (see Use Red Lenses to Sort Colors into Shades, page 32). The colors that are too light or too dark will jump out at you; set those aside. Try to end up with a total of eight to ten shades. Then tie up balls of strips in each of the shades, and designate them as A through H, with A being the very darkest and H the very lightest. (If you have ten shades, assign them letters A through J.) When you design your rug, use the shade pattern in the table (page 79) to blend your shades. In the pattern, each letter represents 1 garter-stitch ridge knit in that shade. So, following the pattern, start with 4 garter-stitch ridges of A. Then 4 ridges in which you alternate A and B. Then 4 ridges of B, followed by 4 ridges in which you alternate B and C. See the pattern? I use this system in a number of my designs, including the Floating Square series here.

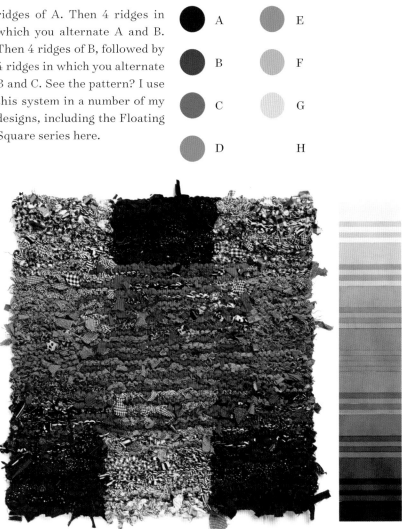

A

B

C

D

E

F

G

H

CHAPTER 5

Tantalizing
Tessellations

Some of my best ideas have come from quilt designers, including Jinny Beyer, who provides quilters with a wealth of design ideas in her fabulous *Designing Tessellations*. In this book she shows how the ancient design concept of tessellation, or repeating, interlocking shapes, can be used in quilt designs. Those same concepts can be used when designing knitted rugs. Beyer does vastly more with the concept than I have been able to manage with garter stitch, which doesn't lend itself to some of the more intricate designs. The designs in this chapter are made from units of mostly the same size and shape, which are repeatedly rotated and/or moved in order to create the patterns.

05 / Blue and Teal Tessellated Rug

This twelve-block rug has been knit in two very different color palettes: one in two shades of red and two of gray (shown in the photo on the facing page), and another with four blocks of dark blue, two of medium blue, four of medium teal, and two of dark teal (at right). In each rug, every color block begins and ends with two black garter-stitches ridges. In the blue and teal rug, the border is worked in narrower blocks knit in the same color-change pattern, outlined on the inner edge with black.

Project Overview

- Each of the twelve blocks has the same stitch and garter-stitch ridge counts. For instructions, see Knitting the Blocks, below.

- For every block, the cast on is the first row of the first garter-stitch ridge, and the second row of the last garter-stitch ridge is the bind off.

- As you complete each block, label it. Following the chart on the opposite page, pin paper labels with the appropriate color on the front side of each block. It is *very* easy to use the wrong block when pinning up, especially if you are pinning under artificial light. Putting the wrong block in the wrong place will ruin the lattice effect.

FINISHED MEASUREMENTS
39" × 30"

KNITTING THE BLOCKS

Knit 12 blocks: four dark blue, two medium blue, two dark teal, and four medium teal, working the following pattern to knit each block.

Setup. Using black, cast on 14 stitches, turn and knit back. (1 garter-stitch ridge)

Next rows. Continuing with black, knit 1 more garter-stitch ridge. (2 black garter-stitch ridges total)

With one of the four colors, knit 8 garter-stitch ridges.

Cut the fabric strip, leaving a 12- to 20-inch tail, and draw the tail through the last stitch to fasten off.

With black, knit 1 garter-stitch ridge, followed by 1 more row and then the bind off. (2 black garter-stitch ridges total)

KNITTING THE BORDERS

The black 2-stitch-wide inner border is knit separately from the outer 4-stitch-wide color-block border. Both the inner and outer borders are knit in four pieces: two for the short sides and two for the long sides. The two color-block short-side borders have black squares at each corner; the long-side color-block borders end on a colored square. The long-side borders are inset between the short-side borders. Pin and stitch the black inner borders to the rug, then attach the color-block borders. For all border pieces, the cast on is the first row of the first garter-stich ridge and the bind off is the second row of the last garter-stitch ridge.

Black inner border (make 2 short-side borders and 2 long-side borders). Cast on 2 and knit back. Knit each border strip until you have 38 garter-stitch ridges for the short sides and 49 garter-stitch ridges for the long sides.

Short-side color-block borders (make 2): Using black, cast on 4, turn, and knit back. Follow the chart on the opposite page for the color order and garter-stitch ridge counts.

Long-side color-block borders (make 2): Using medium blue, cast on 4, turn, and knit back. Follow the chart on the opposite page for the color order and garter-stitch ridge counts.

Starting with the black border pieces, pin the long-side borders to the rug and stitch, being careful to adjust the borders so that the ends of the borders align with the ends of the rug stitches. Then, pin the short-side borders to the short ends of the rug, making sure that the ends of the borders align with the outside edges of the rug.

Next, follow the same procedure to attach the color-block borders to the rug.

ONE BLOCK

← 14 sts →

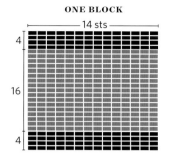

4

16

4

LONG-SIDE
BORDER

← 4 sts →

Bind off

8

2

8

2

8

2

8

2

8

2

8

2

8

2

8

Cast on

SHORT-SIDE
BORDER

← 4 sts →

Bind off

8

8

2

8

2

8

2

8

2

8

2

8

2

8

Cast on

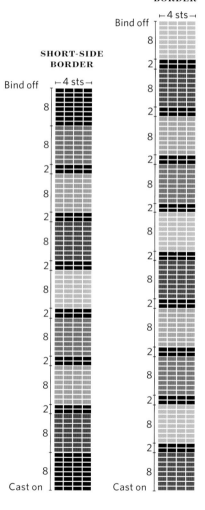

RUG ASSEMBLY

Refer to the watercolor drawing above, and pin units together two at a time. For example, start by pinning, then stitching 2 units together until you've used all of them. Next, pin, then stitch these two-piece units to other two-piece units. Follow this same procedure with the four-piece units, first pinning them all, then stitching them together. Check the drawing regularly as you work. It's important not to pin more than two units together at a time. You wouldn't think it would matter, but it does.

- Dark teal
- Medium teal
- Dark blue
- Medium blue
- Black

1 square = 1 row and 1 stitch

06 / Interlocking Cs

This design is based on tessellation and developed from a quilt squares pattern. In both the quilt and my design, the core unit is a simple rectangular block, but the use of different colors and the way the blocks are rotated and fitted together creates the illusion of interlocking C-shapes. Red is the secret to this design's success; it pops and makes the C shape quite visible.

Project Overview

- Each block consists of two of the colors (color A and color B), plus black in the center. See Color Plan on the opposite page for how many blocks to knit of each color pairing.

- Each of the blocks has the same stitch and garter-stitch ridge counts. For instructions, see Knitting the Squares, on the opposite page.

- For every block, the cast on is the first row of the first garter-stitch ridge, and the second row of the last garter-stitch ridge is the bind off.

- It's important to keep very good track of how many units you complete, or sewing up this rug will be a nightmare (as I know from experience). If you discover you need a particular block in another part of the rug after pieces are sewn together, unpicking the seams is very tedious. The individual units are less interchangeable than you might think, and because the wrong-side garter-stitch ridge "dashes" are painfully visible, you can't flip the pieces over and use the back side.

FINISHED MEASUREMENTS
48" wide × 72" long

Color Plan for Squares

COLOR A	COLOR B	NUMBER OF BLOCKS
Red	Tan	11
Red	Green	15
Purple	Tan	3
Purple	Green	3
Purple	Bright blue	1
Red	Bright blue	5

Color Plan for Triangles

Make all of the increases on every triangle on the same side (the wrong side). Knit the two triangles that make up each corner to the same pattern as all the others. For how to attach the corners to the rug, see next page.

COLOR A	COLOR B	NUMBER OF TRIANGLES
Red	Green	3
Green	Red	8
Tan	Red	2
Bright blue	Red	2
Red	Bright blue	1
Green	Purple	2
Tan	Purple	2

- 🔴 Red
- 🟤 Tan
- 🟢 Green
- 🟣 Purple
- ⚪ Bright blue
- ⚫ Black

KNITTING THE SQUARES

Setup. Using color A, cast on 15 stitches, turn and knit back.

Next rows. Continuing with color A, knit 4 more garter-stitch ridges. (5 garter-stitch ridges total)

With black, knit 2 garter-stitch ridges.

With color B, knit 5 garter-stitch ridges, binding off on the second row of the last garter-stitch ridge (wrong side). Cut the fabric strip, leaving a 12- to 20-inch tail, and draw the tail through the last stitch to fasten off.

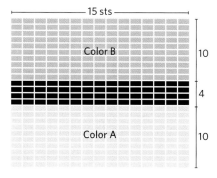

1 square = 1 row and 1 stitch

KNITTING THE TRIANGLES

Setup. Using color A, cast on 1 stitch, turn, kfb, and knit back (1 garter-stitch ridge).

Next rows. Kfb at the beginning of each **wrong-side** row, working garter stitch in the following color progression:

With color A, knit 5 more garter-stitch ridges. (7 stitches and 6 garter-stitch ridges)

With black, knit 2 garter-stitch ridges. (9 stitches)

With color B, knit 5 garter-stitch ridges, binding off on the second row of the last garter-stitch ridge. (wrong side; 13 stitches bound off) Cut the fabric strip, leaving a 12- to 20-inch tail, and draw the tail through the last stitch to fasten off.

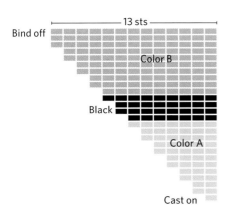

1 square = 1 row and 1 stitch

RUG ASSEMBLY

Refer to the photo (page 90) and the watercolor plan (above), and pin, then stitch 2 units together until you've used all of them. Next, pin and stitch these two-piece units to other two-piece units. Follow this same procedure with the four-piece units, first pinning them all, then stitching them together. Check the chart regularly as you work.

To attach the corners, sew two triangles together so the base of one joins the right-angle edge of the other, then sew each corner piece to one of the long strips of square units before stitching the long strips to each other.

Work additional pieces as needed to fill in and square off the edge.

To develop this idea, I sketched blocks to experiment with creating interlocking shapes without mitering corners, then I worked out the color placement on graph paper. As you can see, there are endless possible color schemes, each resulting in different effects, depending on the colors you choose and what you choose to emphasize as focal points.

CHAPTER 6

Log Cabin

Designs and Beyond

I use the term *log cabin* to distinguish those patterns that are built by changing colors on the diagonal. This is not exactly the same way quilters use the label. Stay with me.

Most of the rugs in this chapter are built in a "cast on 1, increase to desired width, bind off to 1 stitch" module. Colors can change three, five, or seven times across that unit, or not at all. Colors can change abruptly or subtly. Sometimes the unit is a square, and sometimes it's a right triangle. Because the units are small, this is one of the more portable patterns. In simple color systems such as Pink and Yellow on the next page, you don't even need to look at the chart once you learn the color changes.

One of the reasons I chose to knit these squares on the diagonal is that there are fewer cast ons and bind offs than if they were knit as a straight square.

07

Pink and Yellow Log Cabin

Each square in this simple design is knit on the diagonal, starting with yellow at the first corner, increasing to the square's widest point with pink, then beginning to decrease, still in pink followed by a few rows of print fabric, and ending with black at the opposite corner. When you join four units so that four yellow corners abut, new patterns appear. You can detect subtle lines not only at the edges but also where the four units join.

I experimented doing without borders for a few rugs but have since gone back and added them to more than one of my early rugs. The border of Pink and Yellow Log Cabin was an afterthought, but it makes the rug look very much more polished and complete.

Project Overview

- It's important to develop a good system for keeping track of what you've completed, both so that you know what you still need to knit, and so you have a record of where all the pieces go when it's time to assemble them.

- This rug features three solid colors (pink, yellow, and black), plus two or three pink and yellow rayon prints on a black background.

ABBREVIATIONS

kfb — knit in front and back of same stitch

k2tog — knit 2 stitches together

FINISHED MEASUREMENTS

4' wide × 6' long

KNITTING THE RUG
(make 24 identical squares)

Setup. Using yellow, place a slip knot on your left-hand needle, then knit into the back of it to cast on one more stitch. Knit these 2 stitches. (1 garter-stitch ridge)

INCREASE ROWS

With yellow, kfb, knit to end of each row until you have 8 stitches. (4 yellow garter-stitch ridges)

With pink, continue increasing at the beginning of each row until you have 16 stitches. (4 pink garter-stitch ridges)

DECREASE ROWS

With pink, k2tog, knit to end of each row until you have 10 stitches. (7 pink garter-stitch ridges total)

With one of the print fabrics, k2tog, knit to end of each row until you have 6 stitches. (2 print fabric garter-stitch ridges)

With black, k2tog, knit to end of each row until 1 stitch remains.

Cut the fabric strip, leaving a 12- to 20-inch tail, and draw the tail through the last stitch to fasten off.

Assemble the rug following the plan below before knitting the border.

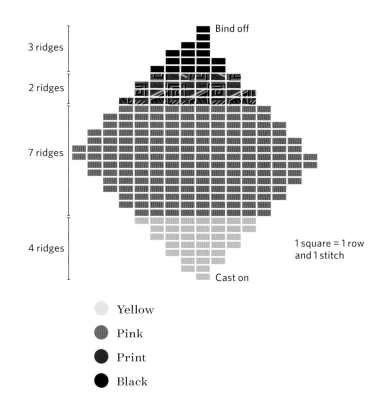

3 ridges

2 ridges

7 ridges

4 ridges

Bind off

Cast on

1 square = 1 row and 1 stitch

Yellow

Pink

Print

Black

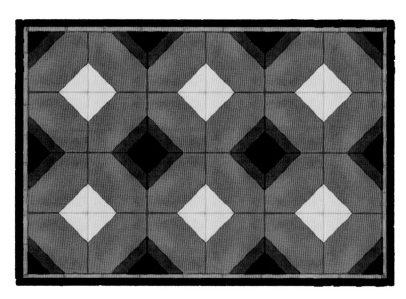

RUG ASSEMBLY

Assemble the rug squares before knitting and adding the borders. Refer to the photo opposite and plan at left, and pin units together two at a time, aligning the colors and stripes, until you've used all of them. Next, pin, then stitch these two-piece units to other two-piece units. Follow this same procedure with the four-piece units, first pinning them all, then stitching them together. Check the plan regularly as you work.

KNITTING THE BORDERS

This rug has two borders: a narrow (2-stitch) pink inner border and a wider (3-stitch) black outer border, knit separately. Both the inner and outer borders are knit in four pieces: two for the short sides and two for the long sides. For all border pieces, the cast on is the first row of the first garter-stitch ridge and the bind off is the second row of the last garter-stitch ridge.

Pink inner border (make 2 short-side borders and 2 long-side borders). Measure the long side of the rug, then knit two border pieces to fit, as follows: Cast on 2 and knit in garter stitch until you achieve the desired measurement for each piece. Pin the long-side borders to the rug and stitch, being careful to adjust the borders so that the ends of the borders align with the ends of the rug. Measure the width of the rug (with the long-side borders attached). Cast on 2, and knit to the desired measurement. Pin the short-side borders to the rug, making sure that the ends of the borders align with the outside edges of the rug.

Black outer border (make 2 short-side borders and 2 long-side borders). Follow the same procedure for measuring as described for the inner border. (The rug will be slightly larger with the inner border now attached.) Cast on 3, and knit in garter stitch until you achieve the desired measurement for each piece. Repeat the process you used for the inner border to attach the outer border.

This blue-and-yellow rug was the second rug I knit. It is knit in triangles, casting on one stitch and increasing, then turning the triangle and picking up stitches to work back in the second colorway. It took only one rug to decide that picking up stitches was not fun. The color play was attractive, however, so subsequent designs, including the shading and stripes, use other knitting techniques.

Don't use light colors on the floor in a high-traffic area. Old T-shirt material picks up and holds dirt, so after this rug provided several years' service in the bathroom, it was retired.

This is very rich design territory, once you figure out if you enjoy knitting the basic unit. It's hard to believe that all of the rugs in this chapter were knit following a similar design approach. It can be really fun to present these as puzzles and confound your friends!

Notice how even though the construction and color palette is the same in the two sketches at the bottom of the page, changing which colors are used where creates a very different design.

08

Blue and Black Log Cabin

Like Pink and Yellow Log Cabin, this rug is composed of squares knit on the diagonal. The color scheme is more complicated than Pink and Yellow, however, making it even more important to keep track of each block by numbering it and checking it off on the plan when you've completed it.

Project Overview

- This rug features three shades of blue (dark, medium, and light), three shades of black-and-white prints (dark, medium, and light), and black. Although the squares have the same stitch and ridge counts, the color patterns differ from block to block (see Color Plan, on the opposite page).

- When you have completed all the squares, assemble the rug following the instructions on page 106, then knit the border.

following the instructions on page 106, then knit the border.

ABBREVIATIONS

kfb — knit in front and back of same stitch

k2tog — knit 2 stitches together

FINISHED MEASUREMENTS
40" wide × 40" long

KNITTING THE BLOCKS

Setup. Using color A, place a slip knot on your left-hand needle, then knit into the back of it to cast on one more stitch. Knit these 2 stitches.

INCREASE ROWS
Continuing with color A, kfb, knit to end of each row until you have 6 stitches. (3 color A garter-stitch ridges total)

Continue to increase by working kfb in the first stitch of each row as follows:

Change to black, and work until you have 8 stitches. (1 black garter-stitch ridge)

Change to color B, and work until you have 12 stitches. (2 color B garter-stitch ridges)

Change to black, and work until you have 14 stitches. (1 black garter-stitch ridge)

DECREASE ROWS
Decrease by working k2tog at the beginning of each row as follows:

Change to color C, and work until you have 10 stitches. (2 color C garter-stitch ridges)

(continued on page 106)

Color Plan

The 36 squares follow the same stitch and garter-stitch ridge counts (see chart below),
knit in six different color patterns.

PATTERN #	NUMBER TO MAKE	COLOR A	COLOR B	COLOR C	COLOR D
1	8	Dark blue	Medium gray	Medium blue	Dark gray
2	4	Medium gray	Dark blue	Light gray	Bright blue
3	4	Medium gray	Dark blue	Dark blue	Dark gray
4	4	Dark gray	Dark blue	Medium gray	Medium blue
5	12	Medium gray	Medium blue	Light gray	Bright blue
6	4	Medium gray	Dark blue	Medium gray	Medium blue
7	4	Medium blue	Medium gray	Light gray	Bright blue

- ● Dark blue
- ● Medium blue
- ● Bright blue
- ● Dark gray
- ● Medium gray
- ○ Light gray
- ● Black

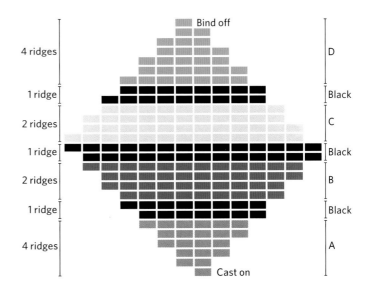

1 square = 1 row and 1 stitch

Change to black, and work until you have 8 stitches. (1 black garter-stitch ridge)

Change to color D, and work until you have 2 stitches. (3 color D garter-stitch ridges)

Next row. K2tog.

Cut the fabric strip, leaving a 12- to 20-inch tail, and draw the tail through the last stitch to fasten off.

Assemble the rug following the plan below before knitting the border.

Assembly Plan

ROW	PATTERN #					
TOP ROW	1	3	4	4	3	1
ROW 2	1	6	5	5	6	1
ROW 3	2	7	5	5	7	2
ROW 4	2	7	5	5	7	2
ROW 5	1	6	5	5	6	1
ROW 6	1	3	4	4	3	1

RUG ASSEMBLY

Pin two units together, aligning the colors and stripes, and sew them up. Pin and stitch as many 2-unit sections as you can before beginning to pin two 2-unit sections to each other.

KNITTING THE BORDER

This rug has two borders: a narrow (2-stitch) black inner border and a wider color-block border. Knit the border pieces after all the squares are completed and assembled. Use the colors you have the most of: in this case, I used bright blue, medium blue, black and white, and dark blue. Each color block is 4 stitches wide and 4 garter-stitch ridges long, with 1 garter-stitch ridge of black between. The borders simply abut; they are not mitered.

Knitting the black border. The inner black border is knit separately from the color block border and in four separate pieces, one for each side. Lay the rug out flat and measure the sides. Using black, cast on 2 stitches, and knit a piece for each side to fit. (See page 44 for advice on how to measure for borders.)

Knitting the color block border. Using bright blue, cast on 4 stitches, turn, and knit back. Follow the color progression in the chart at right.

Attaching the borders. Pin, then stitch the inner black border pieces, allowing the ends to abut. (This rug does not have mitered corners.) Pin, then stitch the four pieces of the color block border, again abutting the ends.

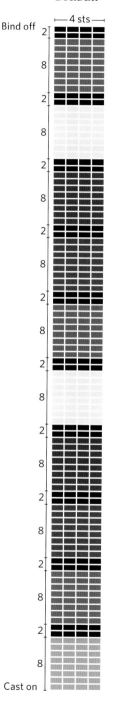

COLOR BLOCK BORDER

Bind off

├─ 4 sts ─┤

Cast on

- ◉ Bright blue
- ◉ Medium blue
- ◉ Dark gray
- ● Dark blue
- ○ Light gray
- ● Black

Note that each 8-row color block is followed by 2 rows of black.

1 square = 1 row and 1 stitch

09

Teal, Purple, Olive, and Ruby Log Cabin

Just as this rug began, I read Jinny Beyer's book *Color Confidence for Quilters,* in which she makes the point that quilters often pull colors from a printed fabric to use as color inspiration for a quilt. However, if they don't also pull the black that is often a border around blocks of color, the quilt will be flat, and the quilter won't know where the problem lies. Jinny had a point: I wasn't thrilled with the way some of my rugs had come out; they weren't as exciting as they should be, given the colors I had available.

I had finished one square for this rug without black and decided to test her theory and make the next one with black borders. The difference was profound. I now keep balls of black fiber tied up at all times, so black is always ready to go and rarely knit anything without using black in the design.

Project Overview

- This rug is composed of seven almost-identical squares knit on the diagonal from corner to corner. The bands of color in each square are knit in the same order, starting with ruby, followed by teal, purple, and olive; each of these colored bands is separated from the next band by 1 garter-stitch ridge of black. When the rug is assembled, there are two shades of the teal: the blocks created by the squares have two dark teal bands and two light teal bands.

- The outer edge of the rug is composed of ten triangles, five of each color pattern. The tricky part of knitting these triangles is making sure you have the colors aligned correctly so that the long side of the triangle is on the outside of the rug, and the color bands match up with those on the inner squares. The two shades of teal are also used in these triangles.

ABBREVIATIONS

kfb — knit into the front and back of the stitch

k2tog — knit two stitches together

FINISHED MEASUREMENTS
34" wide × 52" long

KNITTING THE SQUARES

(make 7 squares; use dark teal for 3 of them and light teal for 4 of them.)

Setup. Using ruby, place a slip knot on your left-hand needle, then knit into the back of it to cast on one more stitch. Knit these 2 stitches.

INCREASE ROWS

Continuing with ruby, kfb, knit to end of each row until you have 14 stitches. (7 ruby garter-stitch ridges total)

Continue to increase by working kfb in the first stitch of each row as follows:

Change to black, and work until you have 16 stitches. (1 black garter-stitch ridge)

Change to teal, and work until you have 24 stitches. (4 teal garter-stitch ridges)

Change to black, and work until you have 26 stitches. (1 black garter-stitch ridge)

DECREASE ROWS

Decrease by working k2tog at the beginning of each row as follows:

Change to purple, and work until you have 18 stitches. (4 purple garter-stitch ridges)

Change to black, and work until you have 16 stitches. (1 black garter-stitch ridge)

Change to olive, and work until 2 stitches remain. (7 olive garter-stitch ridges)

Next row. K2tog.

Cut the fabric strip, leaving a 12- to 20-inch tail, and draw the tail through the last stitch to fasten off.

Knit six more squares following this pattern. Remember to use dark teal for 3 of the squares and light teal for 4 of them.

KNITTING OUTER TRIANGLES

To finish the outside edges of this rug, you will need 10 triangles in four different color transitions. Note that the increases need to be on different sides of the triangle, and because garter stitch has a right and wrong side, the pieces are not reversible.

If you're not sure how this will work for your own colorway, draw up the pattern on a small piece of paper and label what the colors need to be. Cut out the triangles. Count which ones are identical in both colorway *and* straight side.

Triangle A
(make 3)

Setup. Using ruby, place a slip knot on your left-hand needle, then knit into the back of it to cast on one more stitch. Knit these 2 stitches.

INCREASE ROWS
Increase by working kfb at the beginning of each right-side row and knitting to the end of each wrong-side row, as follows:

Continuing with ruby, work until you have 8 stitches. (7 ruby garter-stitch ridges)

Change to black, and work 2 rows. (1 black garter-stitch ridge)

Change to light teal, and work until you have 13 stitches. (4 light teal garter-stitch ridges)

Change to black, and work 2 rows. (1 black garter-stitch ridge)

DECREASE ROWS
Decrease by working k2tog at the beginning of each right-side

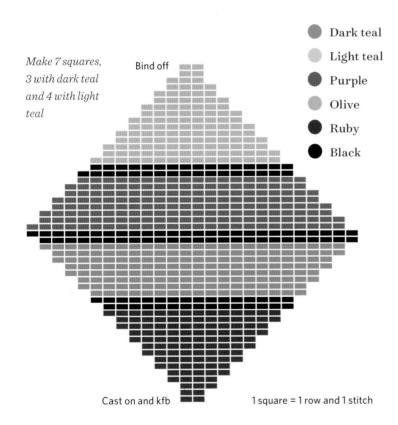

Make 7 squares, 3 with dark teal and 4 with light teal

Bind off

- Dark teal
- Light teal
- Purple
- Olive
- Ruby
- Black

Cast on and kfb   1 square = 1 row and 1 stitch

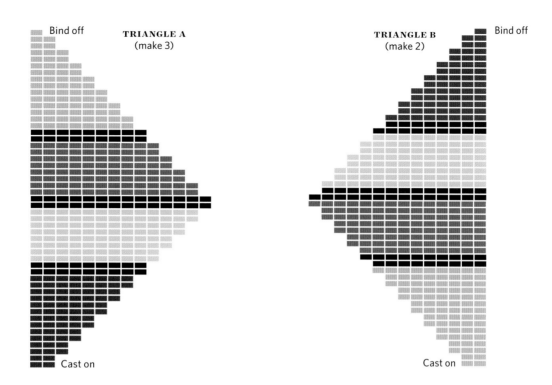

Bind off

TRIANGLE A
(make 3)

Cast on

TRIANGLE B
(make 2)

Bind off

Cast on

row and knitting to the end of each wrong-side row, as follows:

Change to purple, and work until you have 10 stitches. (4 purple garter-stitch ridges)

Change to black, and work 2 rows. (1 black garter-stitch ridge)

Change to olive, and work until 2 stitches remain. (7 olive garter-stitch ridges)

Next row. K2tog.

Leaving a 12- to 20-inch tail, cut the fabric strip, and draw the tail through the last stitch to fasten it off.

Triangle B
(make 2)

Setup. Using olive, place a slip knot on your left-hand needle, then knit into the back of it to cast on one more stitch. Knit these 2 stitches.

INCREASE ROWS

Increase by knitting to the end of each right-side row and working kfb at the beginning of each wrong-side row as follows:

Continuing with olive, work until you have 8 stitches. (7 olive garter-stitch ridges total)

Change to black, and work 2 rows. (1 black garter-stitch ridge)

Change to purple, and work until you have 13 stitches. (4 purple garter-stitch ridges)

Change to black, and work 2 rows. (1 black garter-stitch ridge)

DECREASE ROWS

Decrease by knitting to the end of each right-side row and working k2tog at the beginning of each wrong-side row as follows:

Change to light teal, and work until you have 10 stitches. (4 light teal garter-stitch ridges)

Change to black, and work 2 rows. (1 black garter-stitch ridge)

Change to ruby, and work until until 2 stitches remain. (7 ruby garter-stitch ridges)

Next row. K2tog.

Leaving a 12- to 20-inch tail, cut the fabric strip, and draw the tail through the last stitch to fasten it off.

Triangle C
(make 3)

Setup. Using olive, place a slip knot on your left-hand needle, then knit into the back of it to cast on one more stitch. Knit these 2 stitches.

INCREASE ROWS

Increase by working kfb at the beginning of each right-side row and knitting to the end of each wrong-side row, as follows:

Continuing with olive, work until you have 8 stitches. (7 olive garter-stitch ridges total)

■ Bind off   **TRIANGLE C**
                (make 3)

▨ Cast on   1 square = 1 row and 1 stitch

Change to black, and work 2 rows. (1 black garter-stitch ridge)

Change to purple, and work until you have 13 stitches. (4 purple garter-stitch ridges)

Change to black, and work 2 rows. (1 black garter-stitch ridge)

DECREASE ROWS

Decrease by working k2tog at the beginning of each right-side row and knitting to the end of each wrong-side row, as follows:

Change to dark teal, and work until you have 10 stitches. (4 dark teal garter-stitch ridges)

Change to black, and work 2 rows. (1 black garter-stitch ridge)

Change to ruby, and work until 2 stitches remain. (7 ruby garter-stitch ridges)

Next row. K2tog.

Leaving a 12- to 20-inch tail, cut the fabric strip, and draw the tail through the last stitch to fasten it off.

Triangle D

(make 2)

Setup. Using ruby, place a slip knot on your left-hand needle, then knit into the back of it to cast on one more stitch. Knit these 2 stitches.

INCREASE ROWS

Increase by knitting to the end of each right-side row and working kfb at the beginning of each wrong-side row as follows:

Continuing with ruby, work until you have 8 stitches. (7 ruby garter-stitch ridges total)

Change to black, and work 2 rows. (1 black garter-stitch ridge)

Change to dark teal, and work until you have 13 stitches. (4 dark teal garter-stitch ridges)

Change to black, and work 2 rows. (1 black garter-stitch ridge)

DECREASE ROWS

Decrease by knitting to the end of each right-side row and working kfb at the beginning of each wrong-side row as follows:

Change to purple, and work until you have 10 stitches. (4 purple garter-stitch ridges)

Change to black, and work 2 rows. (1 black garter-stitch ridge)

Change to olive, and work until 2 stitches remain. (7 olive garter-stitch ridges)

Next row. K2tog.

Leaving a 12- to 20-inch tail, cut the fabric strip, and draw the tail through the last stitch to fasten it off.

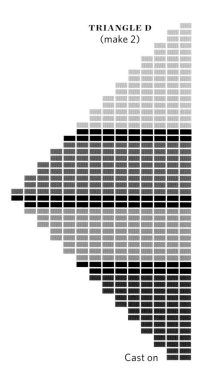

TRIANGLE D
(make 2)

Cast on

This early sketch shows the color plan without the shading on one of the color bands.

RUG ASSEMBLY

Pin two units together, aligning the colors and stripes, and sew them up. Pin and stitch as many 2-unit sections as you can before beginning to pin two 2-unit sections to each other.

KNITTING THE BORDER

This rug is bordered with four 4-stitch-wide strips worked in black; the strips abut at the corners with a mitered seam. To ensure that the mitered corner units fit together correctly, make all increases along the same edge of the piece at one end of the strip and all decreases along the other edge of the opposite end of the strip. To determine the length needed for each side, measure the rug, then work the border pieces as follows.

BORDER PIECES
(make 2 for the long sides and 2 for the short sides)

Cast on 1 stitch, turn, kfb.

Next row (right side). Work even.

Next row (wrong side). Kfb, knit to end.

Repeat these 2 rows until you have 4 stitches.

Knit until the piece measures the correct length for one of the sides, measuring from the shorter side of the border piece (this will be the inner edge of the corner).

Next row (right side). K2tog, knit across.

Next row (wrong side). Knit across.

Repeat these 2 rows until 1 stitch remains. Leaving a 12- to 20-inch tail, cut the fabric strip, and draw the tail through the last stitch to fasten it off.

10

August: Turquoise and Orange

At first glance, this bold design seems quite simple, but subtle details are what make it interesting. Notice that there is a skinny band of pink between the turquoise and the orange on the outside of the rug, and a skinny band of orange between the turquoise center and the smaller pink square on the inside. Also, each of the three major colors — teal, orange, and pink — include shades from lighter to darker, then back again around the rug. The pink on the right side is in fact darker than the pink on the left, and the orange is brighter and lighter on the upper left than on the lower right. (The following directions don't specify this shading; for advice on how to do it, see Artist's Sketchbook on page 123.)

Project Overview

- Each one of the 24 squares that make up the main section of the rug is knit on the diagonal, starting with 1 stitch cast on, increasing to the widest point, then decreasing to 1 on the opposite corner. The widest point is a narrow band of two garter-stitch ridges in a color that contrasts with the two colors of the increasing and decreasing sections of the square.

- There are 24 squares, with three different color progressions: 4 of Block #1, 8 of Block #2, and 12 of Block #3. See table on opposite page for specifics.

ABBREVIATIONS

kfb — knit into the front and back of the stitch

k2tog — knit two stitches together

FINISHED MEASUREMENTS
41" × 41"

KNITTING THE SQUARES

Refer to the Color Progression table on the facing page for color changes and number of squares to knit of each progression.

Cast on. Place a slip knot on your left-hand needle, then knit into the back of it to cast on one more stitch. Knit these 2 stitches.

INCREASE ROWS
Kfb at the beginning of **each row**, and knit across until you have 16 stitches. (8 garter-stitch ridges)

CENTER BAND
Change color, increase as before for 1 garter-stitch ridge, then knit 1 more garter-stitch ridge with the same color and no further increases.

DECREASE ROWS
Change color, k2tog at the beginning of **each row**, and knit to end until 2 stitches remain, k2tog. (8 garter-stitch ridges)

Cut the fabric strip, leaving a 12- to 20-inch tail, and draw the tail through the last stitch to fasten off.

Color Progression

- ◯ Turquoise
- ◉ Pink
- ● Orange

SQUARE #	CAST ON AND INCREASE ROWS	CENTER BAND	DECREASE AND BIND OFF ROWS	NUMBER OF SQUARES
1	Turquoise	Orange	Pink	4
2	Pink	Turquoise	Orange	8
3	Orange	Pink	Turquoise	12

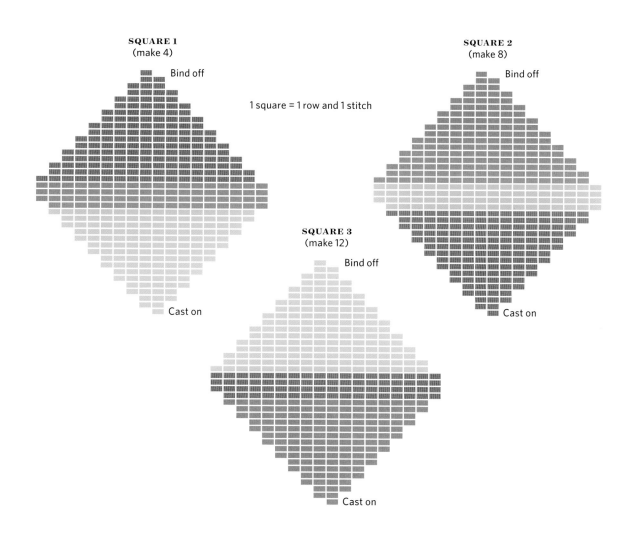

SQUARE 1
(make 4)

Bind off

1 square = 1 row and 1 stitch

Cast on

SQUARE 2
(make 8)

Bind off

Cast on

SQUARE 3
(make 12)

Bind off

Cast on

KNITTING THE TRIANGLES
(make 16)

Setup. Using turquoise, place a slip knot on your left-hand needle, then knit into the back of it to cast on one more stitch. Knit these 2 stitches.

INCREASE ROWS
Kfb at the beginning of **each row**, and knit to end until you have 18 stitches. (9 garter-stitch ridges)

Bind off on the second row of the last garter-stitch ridge. (Remember that your bind-off row will complete the last garter-stitch ridge.)

Cut the fabric strip, leaving a 12- to 20-inch tail, and draw the tail through the last stitch to fasten off.

Note: Label the finished squares as you knit them to help when you assemble the rug.

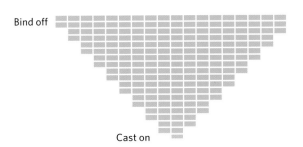

Bind off

Cast on

RUG ASSEMBLY
Pin two units together, aligning the colors and stripes, and sew them together. Pin and stitch as many 2-unit sections as you can before beginning to pin two 2-unit sections to each other to create squares, following the color scheme shown in the watercolor plan at the left. Working on a flat surface, arrange four squares so that one corner of each meets at the center of the rug (A). Starting at the center of the rug, pin two units toether. Stitch. Pin these stitched units to each other along their now longer joint edge. Pin the squares that fill in the corners into their spaces, and stitch (B). Pin, then stitch the triangles to the outer edge.

If you want to shade the rug, as shown in my example, you'll need four shades of each of the three colors. Then knit as follows:

- **Square #1:** One each of the color order turquoise/orange/pink in each of the four shades (four squares in all)

- **Square #2:** Two each of the color order pink/turquoise/orange in each of the four shades (eight squares in all)

- **Square #3:** Three each of the color order orange/pink/turquoise in each of the four shades (twelve squares in all)

- **Triangles:** Four of each of the four shades of turquoise (sixteen triangles in all)

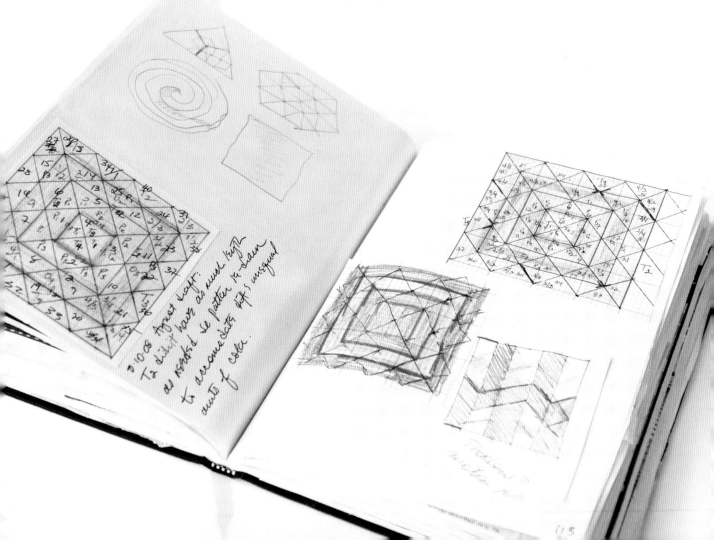

11

Brown and Gray Spiraling Square

The pattern for Spiraling Squares came about when I wondered if it would be possible to "slip" squares around the rug into the next row so that the design looked like it was spiraling. These rugs can be designed so that you create the border as you knit the main pattern.

The concept for this rug is that there are two interlocking spirals: the brown one shading from dark to light at the center and the gray one shading from light to dark at the center. Since these are not in actuality continuous "snakes," the plan for how to achieve the correct shading in the knitted squares must first be worked out on paper.

Project Overview

- Eighteen squares are knit on the diagonal, beginning with the cast on at the first corner, increasing one stitch at the beginning of each row to the center, then decreasing one stitch at the beginning of each row to the bind off at the opposite corner. Six squares are knit "straight" — in other words, from side to side rather than from corner to corner.

- Sixteen triangular units fill in the gaps at the outer edges and form the border of the rug.

- Each of the squares knit on the diagonal is composed of three colors: one of four shades of brown for the cast on and increasing rows, a narrow band of black at the center (one garter-stitch ridge), and one of four shades of gray for the decreasing rows and bind off. The watercolor plan on page 129 shows the color progression from light to dark. Squares with a solid half in one shade are easy: knit 8 garter-stitch ridges of that shade, then work the other shade. The magic comes in the squares that are blended. Here's how to work them:

  SQUARES LABELED 2/1: Knit 5 garter-stitch ridges in shade 2, and 3 garter-stitch ridges in shade 1.

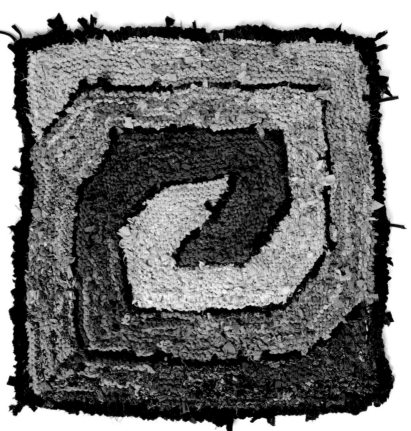

SQUARES LABELED 3/4: Knit 5 garter-stitch ridges in shade 3, and 3 in shade 4.

TRIANGLES: Knit 2 garter-stitch ridges in the main color, then knit 1 ridge of the secondary color alternating with 1 ridge of the main color for 6 garter-stitch ridges. (You will have 8 garter-stitch ridges in all, counting the cast on.) Complete the triangle with 2 garter-stitch ridges of black.

In the photo of Brown-and-Gray Spiraling Square above, you can most clearly see this blending at work in the lower left corner. Everywhere else, the blend is too subtle to detect.

- The last 2 rows of the triangles do not increase and are knit in black to form a self-border.

- Because of the subtlety of the coloring of this design, it's particularly important to keep track of which squares are completed. As you finish each square, pin a number to it that corresponds to your plan, and check it off on the plan.

ABBREVIATIONS

kfb — knit into the front and back of the stitch

k2tog — knit two stitches together

FINISHED MEASUREMENTS

41" × 41"

KNITTING THE SQUARES ON THE DIAGONAL
(make 18)

Refer to the watercolor plan on page 129 for color progression.

Setup. Using one of the browns, place a slip knot on your left-hand needle, then knit into the back of it to cast on 1 more stitch. Knit these 2 stitches.

INCREASE ROWS

Continuing in brown, kfb and knit to end of **each row** until you have 16 stitches. (8 brown garter-stitch ridges)

Change to black, and work 2 rows. (1 black garter-stitch ridge)

DECREASE ROWS

Change to one of the grays, k2tog, and knit to end of **each row** until 2 stitches remain.

Next row. K2tog.

Cut the fabric strip, leaving a 12- to 20-inch tail, and draw the tail through the last stitch to fasten off.

Mark this square complete on your plan.

KNITTING THE "STRAIGHT" SQUARES
(make 6)

The squares outlined in orange on the chart are knit as straight squares. Refer to the watercolor plan (page 129) for color progression.

Using black, cast on 11 stitches, turn, and knit back. (1 black garter-stitch ridge)

For 4 squares, switch to the desired color, and knit every row until you have 10 garter-stitch ridges.

For 2 more squares, switch to black for the last row and bind off. (1 black garter-stitch ridge)

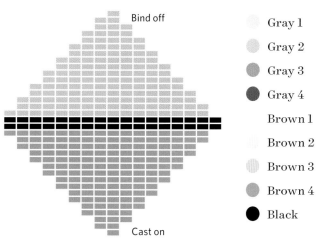

SQUARE ON THE DIAGONAL
(make 18)

Bind off

Cast on

- Gray 1
- Gray 2
- Gray 3
- Gray 4
- Brown 1
- Brown 2
- Brown 3
- Brown 4
- Black

1 square = 1 row and 1 stitch

Once I finished Brown and Gray Spiraling Square, I couldn't help but wonder what would happen if a spiraling square started with both light colors in the middle. The result was Green and Purple Spiraling Square, a rug in eight shades, from dark to light. The sketch at lower right shows how I tested the color shift to see how the different shades would align. I wanted to know where the dark would end up, based on how the colors started in the center of the rug. As it turned out, starting with lights in the middle resulted in a dark border all the way around the rug, which I liked.

The rug was big enough that I let the four corners end on their knitted diagonal, rather than knitting triangles to finish the rug to square.

KNITTING THE TRIANGLES

(make 16)

The triangles around the outer edges are knit as "half units" following the color pattern used for the squares knit on the diagonal.

Setup. Using the color shown on the watercolor plan, place a slip knot on your left-hand needle, then knit into the back of it to cast on 1 more stitch. Knit these 2 stitches.

INCREASE ROWS

Continuing in the color pattern, kfb and knit to end of **each row** until you have 16 stitches. (8 garter stitch ridges)

Change to black, and work 2 rows. (1 black garter-stitch ridge)

Knit 1 row without increasing, bind off on the return.

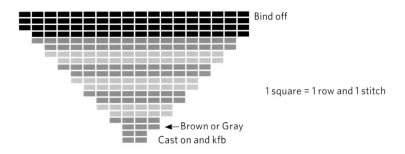

Bind off

1 square = 1 row and 1 stitch

← Brown or Gray
Cast on and kfb

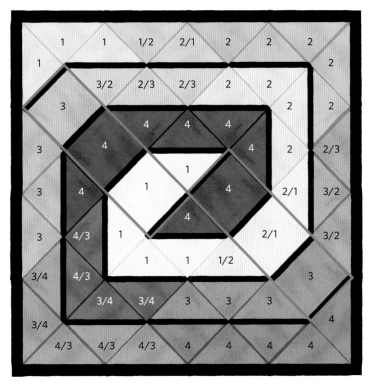

RUG ASSEMBLY

Following the watercolor plan, pin, then stitch one diagonally knit square to one straight-knit square for the center of the rug. Pin and stitch the other pair of diagonally and straight-knit squares that complete the center. Pin and stitch a pair of squares that will be adjacent to one of the sides of the center square, then pin and stitch that unit to the center square. Continue in this manner, building pairs of squares and attaching them around the center square. Use the remaining diagonally knit squares to fill in at the center of each side. Complete the rug by pinning and stitching the triangles in around the edge.

12 / Dancing Triangles

Derived from a quilt pattern, Dancing Triangles is knit completely of right triangles with a purple base, a black stripe, and a lime green top. I like the pattern, but it's a difficult rug to knit. Colorwise, it's the most daring rug in my collection. No one is neutral about this color palette! It's possible there's a lot more colorwork that could be done with this pattern.

Project Overview

- Each of the six bold units of this rug is created by knitting four right-angle triangles, joining them into squares, then joining all six squares together.

- Each triangle is identical, beginning with one stitch and increasing at the beginning of right-side rows to the bind off. The first portion of the triangle is knit in lime green, and the base is knit in purple, with one garter-stitch ridge of black separating the two colors at the center.

- The second row of the last garter-stitch ridge is the bind off.

ABBREVIATIONS

kfb — knit into the front and back of the stitch

k2tog — knit two stitches together

FINISHED MEASUREMENTS

33" wide × 47" long

KNITTING THE TRIANGLES
(make 24)

Setup. Using lime green, place a slip knot on your left-hand needle, then knit into the back of it to cast on one more stitch. Knit these 2 stitches.

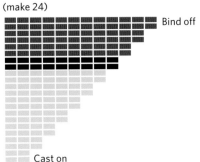

(make 24)

Bind off

Cast on

● Lime green

● Purple

● Black

1 square = 1 row and 1 stitch

INCREASE ROWS

Increase by working kfb at the beginning of each right-side row and knitting to the end of each wrong-side row, as follows:

Continuing with lime green, work until you have 8 stitches. (7 lime green garter-stitch ridges total)

Change to black, and work 2 rows. (1 black garter-stitch ridge)

Change to purple, and work until you have 11 stitches. (2 garter-stitch ridges)

Next row. Kfb, and knit to end.

Bind off, creating the last garter-stitch ridge. (3 purple garter-stitch ridges total)

Cut the fabric strip, leaving a 12- to 20-inch tail, and draw the tail through the last stitch to fasten off.

RUG ASSEMBLY

To assemble, pin four triangles together to form a square, with the purple in the center. Sew them together. Make six squares. Pin, then sew the six squares together.

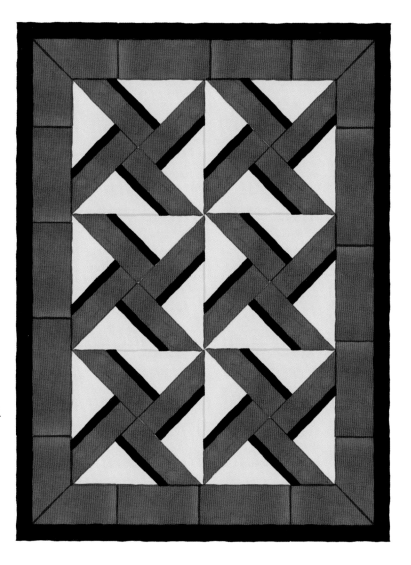

KNITTING AND ATTACHING BORDER

Knit the border after all the squares are completed and assembled. The border is knit in rectangular sections, and attached to the finished rug with the garter-stitch ridges parallel to the edge. Eight corner sections have increases along one edge so that when assembled with these diagonal edges abutting, they form miters for the corners.

Most of the rectangular sections are 12 stitches in length, but you will need to knit some sections on each side narrower or wider to get the right fit.

Work the Corner Border Sections first, then position them on the rug so that the diagonal edges abut to form miters. Pin them to the rug. Do not sew them to the rug yet.

Measure the longest side of one of the corner pieces to determine your approximate gauge over 12 stitches. Then measure the distance between the corner pieces on each of the four sides. Divide each of those measurements by your gauge. This gives you the number of Rectangular Border Sections you'll need to knit. You're unlikely to get an even number, so make one or more pieces narrower (or wider) as needed in order to fill the space.

Once you have knit all the pieces you need to fill the gap on one side of the rug, you may choose to stop and pin them together and to the rug, then stitch. Or you can wait until you have all the pieces done.

CORNER BORDER SECTION #1
(make 4)

Setup. Using purple, cast on 8 stitches, turn and knit back. (1 purple garter-stitch ridge)

Increase by working kfb in the last stitch of each right-side row and working even on wrong-side rows, as follows.

Continuing with purple, work until you have 12 stitches. (5 purple garter-stitch ridges)

Change to black, and work 2 rows, then knit 1 more row, and bind off. (2 black garter-stitch ridges; the bind off forms the second row of the last garter-stitch ridge)

CORNER BORDER SECTION #2
(make 4)

Setup. Using purple, cast on 8 stitches, turn, and knit back. (1 purple garter-stitch ridge)

Increase by working kfb in the first stitch of each right-side row and working even on wrong-side rows, as follows:

Continuing with purple, work until you have 12 stitches. (5 purple garter-stitch ridges)

Change to black, and work 2 rows, then knit 1 more row, and bind off. (1 black garter-stitch ridge; the bind off forms the second row of the last garter-stitch ridge)

RECTANGULAR BORDER SECTION

Make as many as necessary. You may need to make one on each side a few stitches longer or shorter than the directions below specify in order to get the correct length. As usual, the cast on is the first row of the first garter-stitch ridge and the bind off is the second row of the last garter-stitch ridge.

Setup. Cast on (about) 12 stitches in purple.

Knit 5 purple garter-stitch ridges.

Change to black, knit 3 rows, then bind off. (2 black garter-stitch ridges)

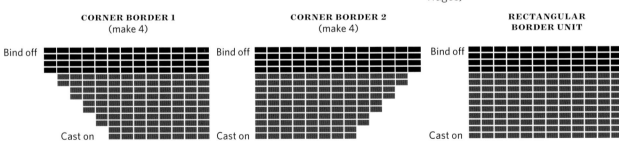

CORNER BORDER 1
(make 4)

Bind off

Cast on

CORNER BORDER 2
(make 4)

Bind off

Cast on

RECTANGULAR BORDER UNIT

Bind off

Cast on

1 square = 1 row and 1 stitch

The quilt pattern this design is based on started my thinking. I didn't want to knit squares and lots of triangles, but I could knit four right triangles pretty easily. I tested the design on graph paper to see how many squares would be needed to make a decent-size rug. Twelve was too many, but six looked like it would work. My notes remind me that I thought about knitting the triangles in three colors but was concerned that there might not be enough contrast for a clear pattern to show up. I was probably right about that.

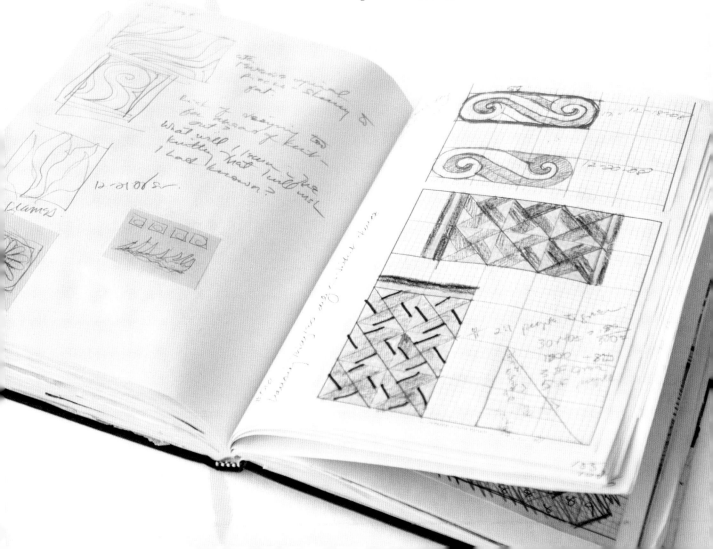

CHAPTER 7

Spirited
Spirals

Inspiration for spiral rugs came from a pattern in Kay Gardiner and Ann Shayne's *Mason-Dixon Knitting*. It was knit as a single strip, and the authors commented on how hard it was to get the strip to lie flat as it spiraled. The solution jumped out: "short rows!" And another new rug was born. In addition to using short rows, I discovered that by knitting three or more strips, these colors could be manipulated much more than if I knit only one strip. How you manage color transitions can have a remarkable effect on the overall design of the rug. Most of the single spirals use three different colorways: a light, a medium, and a dark.

It doesn't matter what form of increase you use to change the width of the strip. In the light of the overall rug and the size of the stitches, any individual shaping becomes invisible. In addition, whether or not any one of the strips has exactly the right number of rows, or whether the short rows are spaced exactly evenly is also not really important. Garter-stitch fabric stretches easily, and the gauge is so large and the raw material so variable that any individual variation will be lost in the overall creation.

Some Basics on Knitting Circular Rugs

Circular rugs are no more difficult to knit than striped rugs or rugs based on quilt designs. They do require a few different techniques, however, including how to calculate yardage requirements, how to work short rows so that they lie flat, and how to assemble the parts so that the rug lies flat.

Calculating Materials for Circular Rugs

Keeping in mind that I estimate 60 yards of sliced fiber per square foot of finished rug, use some math from geometry class to calculate the area of circles: r is the radius (half the diameter) of a circle. Pi, or π, is equal to 3.1416. Here are some examples of how to use the formula for the area of a circle (πr^2) to calculate how much fiber you'll need:

- For a 4-foot-diameter circular rug, where r = 2, the area is 12.5 square feet ($3.1416 \times 2 \times 2 = 12.5$). Multiply 12.5 × 60 yards to get a total of 750 yards; 250 in each colorway if you are making a three-color spiral.
- For a 3-foot-diameter circular rug, where r = 1.5, the area is 7 square feet ($3.1416 \times 1.5 \times 1.5$). Multiply 7 × 60 yards to get a total of 420 yards; 140 yards in each colorway.

Working a Short Row

Short rows are used in knitting to make one edge of a piece of knitting longer than the opposite edge, and they have several useful purposes in these rugs. First, short rows in the arms of a spiral make the arm curve on its own, because the outside edge is longer than the inside edge. This helps the section to lie flat on the floor. In addition, you don't have to compress the inner edge of a strip and stretch the outer edge.

In free-form knitting, such as Green and Pink Ladders (page 162) and Pink Swish (page 168), short rows are used to make otherwise straight sections of knitting move and morph into curves.

I like to work one full-length row in between each of the short rows. In addition, alternate short short rows with long short rows, so that the wrap-and-turns don't align vertically. For example, if you knit 3 stitches before your wrap-and-turn in one short row, knit 4 or 5 stitches before your wrap-and-turn in the next short row. It's a painful feeling to look at a finished rug and notice accidental stripes that appeared because all your short rows are turned at the same place.

That said, several short short rows will put more curve into an outer edge than the same number of long short rows. Most of the time, the rug will tell you what it needs, and when it doesn't, use your own judgment and experiment a bit until you get something that works for you.

WRAP-AND-TURN

A.

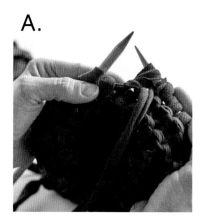

B.

C.

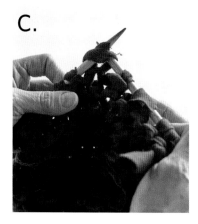

To ensure that there's no hole where you turn to make the short row, use a technique known as "wrap-and-turn." Starting on the "longer" side of the curve (depending on the rug,

this can be front or back), knit a few stitches across the row.

Bring the fiber to the front of the work (A), slip the next stitch purlwise to the right (working) needle (B), pass

the fiber to the back of the work, slip the stitch back to the left-hand needle, turn the work, and knit back (C). Short row completed.

Keep in Mind . . .

- The strips not only need short rows to help them lie flat, but they also taper from one end to the other, so you will be making increases at the same time you are working short rows. To ensure that the knitted strip spirals correctly, it's important to mark the side where you make the increases, so that you can be sure to keep every increase along the same edge. Large quilter's basting safety pins make good markers.

- Leave long, dangly fabric strips when you change colors or end a bind off. These ends will be waiting for you in the right colors to use when it's time to sew up.

- To estimate whether you have enough left to knit one more row when you're getting to the end of your fiber ball, allow three times the length of a row to knit another complete row, and four times the length of a row to work the bind off.

- When I finish a planned rug, I often have extra tied-up strips left over. Rather than untying and throwing them away, or designing a new rug to use up the leftovers, I simply knit out what's left into a small spiral. Round rugs are always the right size. I divide the leftover yarn into two balls and knit each from the cast-on into the middle, and in this way manage to use up all the fiber strips.

Getting Started

Each strip begins with a chain, which creates the narrow taper at the end. If you're a crocheter and have a big enough hook, you can work the first segment of each of the spiral strips by simply crocheting a chain of the required number of stitches. If crocheting isn't your thing, it's easy to create a chain on knitting needles simply by using a knitted cast on (see page 38). Cast on the required number of stitches for the chain, then put the last cast-on stitch on a new needle, and let all the other stitches drop off. Don't worry: they form a chain just like a crocheted chain, and they won't unravel. You can also make the chain using just your fingers.

Assembling Spiral Rugs

When you've finished knitting each of the fabric strips for a spiral rug, lay them out on the floor, bed, or dining room table. (Protect the table if you're using pins that could scratch a finish.) Start pinning the spiral from the inside, and work toward the outside. The outer edges of each strip (where you made all the increases and short rows) should all be toward the outer edge of the rug. (It helps if the dogs stay outside during this exercise.)

Pin the strips along their edges. It takes a lot of pins. Lots. And lots. I don't like to sew anything not pinned at least every 3 inches. If you don't have enough pins, you can put the pins close together in the section you'll sew first, and 6 to 8 inches apart farther ahead, then move pins from the sewn section into the next section you'll be working on. (If you do this, move the pins with the rug flat on a surface, *not* draped across your lap. It's very easy to pin in wrinkles and other unevenness if the rug is not flat.)

Colors of India

Colors of India is a big spiral rug, 48 inches across, with six strips and a black border. The colors were inspired by a picture of a spice market in India. I based the width of the strips on the amount of raw fiber I had in each colorway: lots of red, but only a little purple. Were I to sew it up again, I would not put the yellow right next to the red. Red runs, *always,* and yellow shows it. Had I sewn yellow in between pink and green instead, any bleeding the red did would have been less visible. To make this rug, follow the basic instructions for Black, Gray, and White Spiral (page 142). Knit two tapered strips of each of the six colors, and stitch them together as described.

Sew the strips together using fiber strip tails in colors that blend with adjacent sections. Thread the strips through a needle with the biggest eye you can find. Knitted fabric strips without seams work best for sewing up. Weave in the ends at the start and end of each strip. (Follow the instructions on page 43 for how to stitch.)

I find it works better to start pinning from the inside of the spiral, then sewing from the outside toward the center. The rugs I've sewn from the outside in lie flatter than the ones that I started sewing from the middle. Even if a somewhat large gap appears when you get to the middle, garter stitch will stretch, and you can pull the strips together to fill in the gap with stitches.

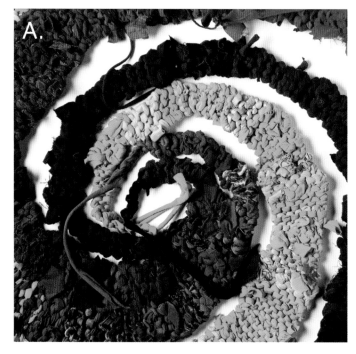

Lay out your knitted strips roughly at first, pushing them around and together to coax them into interlocking spirals (A). When you're satisfied with the result, begin pinning the pieces together, working from the center out (B). Don't forget to use lots of pins!

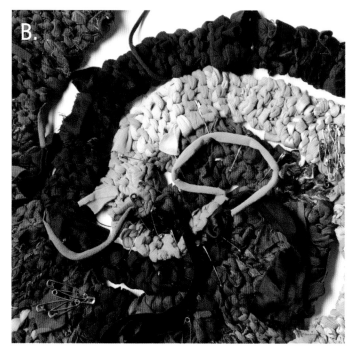

13 / Black, Gray, and White Spiral Rug

Use the basic instructions given here for Black, Gray, and White Spiral for any number of different color combinations, or even different numbers of strips.

Project Overview

- Prepare the fabric for this rug by making four roughly equal-size balls of each of three colors: black, gray blend, and black-and-white blend. You will knit three strips, each of which tapers at both ends. The reason for making four balls of each color is that you use two balls to knit half a strip, bind off, knit an identical strip for the other half of the strip with the second pair of balls of that color, then stitch the two halves of the strip together along the bound-off edge. This ensures that you have enough fabric of each color to complete the strip. *Note:* It's easier to make the tapers at the cast-on end of the strip.

- Take care to make all of the increases on one edge of the strip. This is the same edge where you begin all of the short rows as well. (For how to work short rows, see page 138.)

- Knit six strips, two of each color. If you include high-contrast color changes in these strips (or if you are particularly discerning about the "dotted line" of a wrong-side garter-stitch ridge change), make sure to make your increases on the opposite edge of the second arm. If you are doing gentle shading transitions, it will be almost impossible to spot wrong-side color changes in these spiral rugs.

FINISHED MEASUREMENTS
46" diameter

FIRST HALF STRIP

Setup. Using one of the three colors, make a slip knot and chain 9 (see More than One Way to Chain, see page 147).

Row 1. Holding the needle with the 1 stitch in your left hand, kfb.

Row 2. Work even. (1 garter-stitch ridge)

Work even (no further increases) until you have 9 garter-stitch ridges of 2 stitches.

Next row. Kfb, K1. (3 stitches)

Work even (no further increases) until you have 9 garter-stitch ridges of 3 stitches.

SHORT-ROW SEGMENT #1
Row 1. Kfb, knit to end, turn, and knit back. (4 stitches)

Work even (no further increases) until you have 4 garter-stitch ridges of 4 stitches.

First short row. Starting at the same edge where you have been making the increases, K2, wrap-and-turn (see Wrap-and-Turn, page 139), and knit back. This is the first short row; mark it with a pin.

Work even for 4 more garter-stitch ridges. (9 garter-stitch ridges of 4 stitches, with the short row and its return in the middle)

Repeat Short-Row Segment #1 until you have 8 stitches. Mark the last row with a pin.

SHORT-ROW SEGMENT #2
Work even on these 8 stitches for 6 more garter-stitch ridges.

Second short row. Starting at the same edge where you have been making the increases, K4, wrap-and-turn, and knit back.

Work even (no further increases), inserting a short row every 7th ridge (6 ridges between short rows), until you have used up half of the fiber you prepared in this colorway. In subsequent short rows, stagger the placement of the wrap-and-turn (after 4, 5, or 6 stitches), so that the wrap-and-turn points do not align.

Bind off on the second row of the last garter-stitch ridge. Cut the fabric strip, leaving a 12- to 20-inch tail, and draw the tail through the last stitch to fasten off.

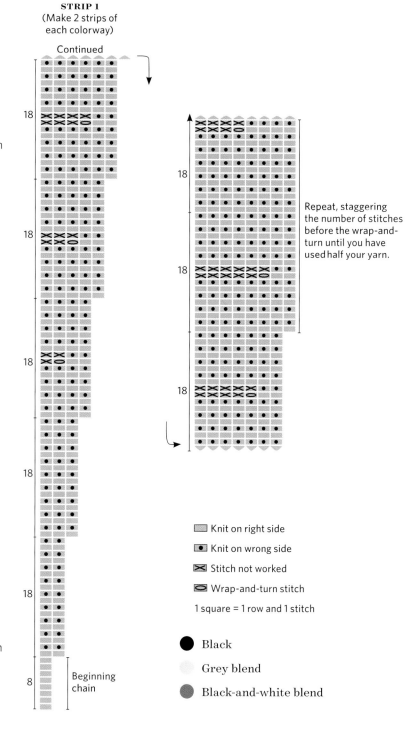

STRIP 1
(Make 2 strips of each colorway)

Continued

18

18

18

18

18

18

8

Beginning chain

18

18

18

18

Repeat, staggering the number of stitches before the wrap-and-turn until you have used half your yarn.

▨ Knit on right side

⊡ Knit on wrong side

⊠ Stitch not worked

⬭ Wrap-and-turn stitch

1 square = 1 row and 1 stitch

● Black

○ Grey blend

● Black-and-white blend

ARTIST'S SKETCHBOOK

The spiral rug shown in the sketch features three 8-stitch-wide strips of garter stitch, tapered at each end. These long strips feature regularly spaced short rows to encourage the strips to curl in a spiral shape. The red, tan, and black rug in the photo has four strips.

SECOND HALF STRIP

Knit a second strip exactly like the first half: same colorway, same increases, and same short rows. Knit until you run out of fiber, then bind off.

KNITTING STRIPS #2 AND 3

Make four more half strips (two of each of the remaining colors), following the preceding directions for the first and second half strips.

ASSEMBLING THE RUG

Stitch each half of the same-colored pairs pieces together along the bound-off edges so that the joined strip is roughly C-shaped.

Starting at the center, pin the long edges of your strips, following the layout. It helps a little if the strips are all roughly the same length, but a foot or two difference over the total length of 20 or 24 feet doesn't matter too much, especially if the colors aren't very high contrast.

Starting at the outer edge, stitch the strips together. (See Assembling Spiral Rugs, page 140, for further information.)

More than One Way to Chain

- If you're a crocheter and have a big enough hook, you can work the first segment of each of the spiral strips by simply crocheting a chain of the required number of stitches.

- If crocheting isn't your thing, it's easy to create a chain on knitting needles simply by using a knitted cast on (see page 38). Cast on the required number of stitches for the chain, then put the last cast-on stitch on a new needle, and let all the other stitches drop off. Don't worry: they won't unravel; they actually form a chain.

- You can also make the chain using just your fingers.

14

Triple Spirals

Not long after I figured out how to knit a single spiral, I started playing with triskele, or triple spiral, patterns. Aidan Meehan uses the triskele in all of his books on designing Celtic knotwork. The first several attempts did not give me anything that looked knittable, but I kept sketching.

The more shading you can work into these rugs, the more interesting they get. The trick is to remember that all shading has to be evenly divided by three (for each of the arms of the triple spiral) and distributed among the tied-up balls before you start. Of course, if getting an even balance of color among the spirals isn't that important to you, or if you'd rather be completely random, then you don't have to worry about this.

When you look closely at this rug, you can see how *very* rich the tweedy accents are. I selected these colors by including *all* of the accent colors suggested in my home paint selector book. For example, whereas the book suggested two accent colors for each brown, I used all of them in small amounts. The overall color of the rug is brown, but look — it contains blue, pink, peach, yellow, purple, and lots of various shades of green. Because of these subtle additions, the rug will work well with many different color schemes.

Project Overview

- The triple spiral rug starts the same as a single spiral: in this case, six garter-stitch strips, tapered to grow from one cast-on stitch to eight, with short rows every six to nine rows (depending on where you are within the taper). The short rows are always along the same side as the increases.

- Unlike the basic spiral (pages 142–47), when you create a triple spiral rug, you join the two half-strips so that the short rows are on opposite sides, thus encouraging half the strip to curve in one direction and the other half in the other direction in a roughly S shape. (Note: Right side of the knitting faces up on both halves.)

- In Brown Triple Spiral, each strip starts with dark brown, then blends through medium shades to a very light shade. To knit this rug, you must knit three half strips with dark brown blending to medium brown and three half strips with light brown blending to medium brown. When you assemble the rug, you join one of the dark-to-medium strips to one of the light-to-medium strips, then join two other pairs in the same way. You then assemble the three joined strips as shown in the plan (see page 152).

- The edges of triple spiral rugs are evened out by knitting gussets (triangles) to fill the gaps (see plan, page 152).

- To estimate how much yardage you'll need for a triple spiral rug, refer to Calculating Materials for Circular Rugs, page 138.

Brown Triple Spiral

KNITTING THE FIRST HALF STRIP

(make 3)

Follow the stitch count, increase, and short-row instructions for First Half Strip of Black, Gray, and White Spiral Rug (starting on page 144), casting on with dark brown and blending gradually to medium brown at the bind off.

KNITTING THE SECOND HALF STRIP

(make 3)

Follow the stitch count, increase, and short row instructions for Second Half Strip of Black, Gray, and White Spiral Rug (page 147), casting on with light brown and blending gradually to medium brown at the bind off.

ASSEMBLING A TRIPLE SPIRAL RUG

Step 1. Lay the strips out on the floor, bed, or a protected dining room table. Working from the inside of each separate spiral and beginning first with the three First Half Strips (dark brown to medium brown), arrange each strip so that the outside edge faces the outside of the rug. Take care not to let the narrow tapered end get twisted. You may need an hour or two of uninterrupted time where you can

Calculating Strip Lengths

When you have a good portion of your rug knit and you want to know, for example, how much longer the outer arms need to be in order to be of equal lengths, lay your pieces out on the floor, bed, or table, depending on what space you have to work with. I don't recommend pinning or, even worse, sewing up, any part of the rug at this stage. I've learned from experience that sewing up too early only leads to having to undo what I've done.

work without having to put everything away before you're finished pinning it all together. You're going to lay all the pieces out in rough fashion before beginning to pin them together.

Step 2. Lay the three Second Half Strips (light brown to medium brown) so that their bound-off edges abut and the two halves spiral in opposite directions. The increases of the Second Half Strips should be on the opposite side from those of the First Half Strip, so that the increases for both

strips face toward the outside of the rug.

Step 3. Work with each pair of strips so that they interlock as shown in the plan below. Check to be sure none of the tapered ends is twisted, and push the pieces snug against each other.

Step 4. Pin the pairs of arms together at the bound-off edges, then stitch them together.

Step 5. Starting at the centers of each spiral, pin the strips together along their edges. Be sure to space

the pins close together and use lots of pins. Note that the center of a triple spiral is stretchy, because it's where three wide parts of garter stitch come together. You can usually pull it together to make it fit, which is better than if it were bunched up because of too much fabric.

Step 6. Once everything is neatly pinned together, begin stitching the strips together, working from the outside in. Pull the three strips together in the center to fill any gap.

gusset

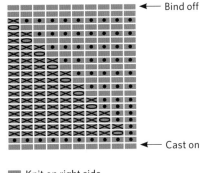

(make 3)

← Bind off

← Cast on

■ Knit on right side

■• Knit on wrong side

✕ Stitch not worked

◎ Wrap-and-turn stitch

1 square = 1 row and 1 stitch

● Dark brown blending to medium brown

● Light brown blending to medium brown

KNITTING THE GUSSETS

(make 3)

Setup. Place a slip knot on your left-hand needle, then knit into the back of it to cast on 1 more stitch. Knit these 2 stitches.

Increase rows. Kfb and knit to end of **each row** until you have 10 stitches.

Finishing. Bind off, creating the last garter-stitch ridge. Cut the fabric strip, leaving a 12- to 20-inch tail, and draw the tail through the last stitch to fasten off.

Fit the triangles into the gaps and sew them in place.

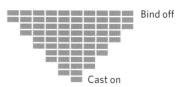

Bind off

Cast on

This rug features a very different color combination from Brown Triple Spiral.

15 / Red Nautilus

I wish there were a better way to knit a nautilus shape, as well as how to get it to curl more precisely into the Fibonacci sequence. I sketch and I knit, and I knit and I sketch, and I go around in spirals. The rugs take a lot of time to finish, but they are beautiful. Each of three nautilus rugs I've knit has required a lot of manual, "lay it out on the floor and decide to knit more" figuring out. You may enjoy experimenting with your own approach.

Project Overview

- All of the Nautilus rugs are knit following the basic spiral arm pattern.

- Red Nautilus has three bands of slightly different-colored reds, plus black.

FINISHED MEASUREMENTS
47" × 38"

ABBREVIATIONS
kfb — Knit into the front and back of the same stitch

KNITTING A NAUTILUS
(make 3)

Setup. Make a slip knot and chain 6. (See More than One Way to Chain, page 147.)

Row 1. Kfb in the 1 stitch on the needle, turn and knit back. (1 garter-stitch ridge of 2 stitches completed)

Next rows. Work even (no further increases) until you have 6 garter-stitch ridges of 2 stitches.

Increase row. Kfb, knit to end, turn and knit back. (3 stitches)

Next rows. Work even until you have 6 garter-stitch ridges of 3 stitches.

SHORT-ROW SEGMENT
Increase row. Kfb, knit to end, turn and knit back. (4 stitches)

Work even until you have 9 garter-stitch ridges of 4 stitches.

Short row. Starting at the same edge on which you have been making the increases, K2, wrap-and-turn, and knit back. Mark this short row with a pin.

Work even until you have 4 more garter-stitch ridges. (14 garter-stitch ridges of 4 stitches in all, including the short row and its return in the middle)

Repeat this Short-Row Segment four more times, until you have 8 stitches. Stagger the short rows

throughout. (85 garter-stitch ridges and 5 short rows)

Note: You can continue to work this pattern until you have 12 stitches if you wish. The wider you make the stripes at the end, the more rectangular the overall proportions of your rug will be.

Bind off on the second row of the last garter-stitch ridge. Cut the fabric strip, leaving a 12- to 20-inch tail, and draw the tail through the last stitch to fasten off.

BORDER STRIP

Using black, cast on 2 stitches. Knit every row until piece is long enough to spiral from the center to form a border.

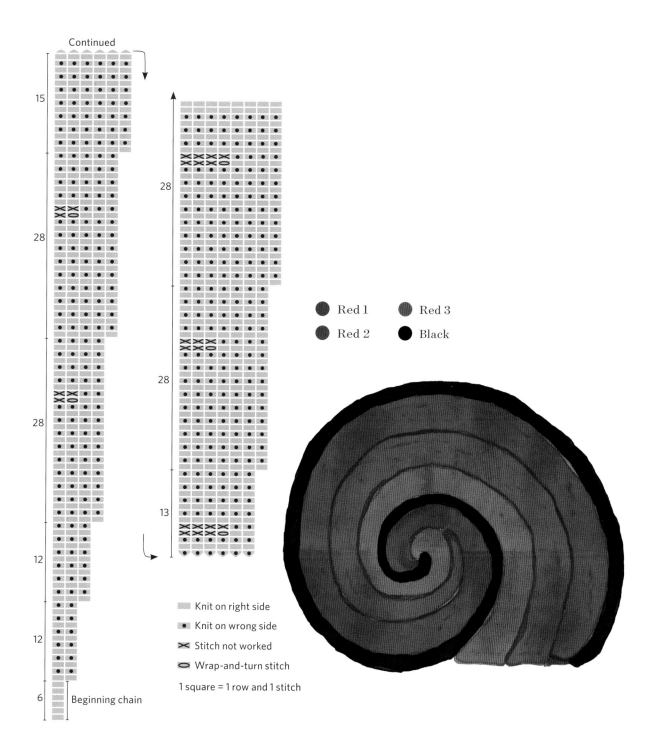

Continued

15

28

28

28

12

12

6   Beginning chain

28

28

28

13

● Red 1   ● Red 3
● Red 2   ● Black

▨ Knit on right side

• Knit on wrong side

✕ Stitch not worked

◯ Wrap-and-turn stitch

1 square = 1 row and 1 stitch

CHAPTER 8

Inspiration
Going Free-Form

The rugs in this chapter are free-form; that is, they don't exactly fit the pattern categories described earlier in the book: stripes, tessellations, log cabins, and spirals, though they do make use of many of the techniques used there. Rather than give you complete directions for how to make these rugs, I'm first going to share some tips, learned by experience, that give better results when designing a free-form rug. Many of these suggestions are just as applicable to all rug knitting, not just free-form patterns. Use these rugs as inspiration for creating your own designs.

Free-Form vs. Freestyle

WORK YOUR DESIGNS OUT ON PAPER before you put your stitches onto needles. Even though the design is *free-form,* it's much better not to *knit freestyle.*

PRESELECT YOUR COLORS, arrange them by shade, and tie up balls of each shade before you start knitting.

EVENLY CUT STRIPS will give you a better chance of getting straight edges on your rugs.

COUNT RIDGES instead of measuring with a tape. Pieces will stretch, but the count of garter-stitch ridges will not vary. Because garter stitch is so regular, it's very easy to get whatever size you want, so that pieces are consistent when you go to match them and sew up.

REMEMBER THAT, IF YOU ARE CHANGING COLORS, garter stitch creates a different look on the front and back side of a piece. This is particularly noticeable if you're working with highly contrasting colors and aren't disciplined about keeping all of your color changes on the same side of the pieces.

TRY TO ENSURE THAT YOU HAVE ENOUGH OF EACH SHADE of the fabric strips you'll be knitting with. If you have to find and cut up more midproject, it will probably be difficult to get an exact match.

Pastel Plaid is an example of what happens when you don't develop the design on paper before starting to knit. Its "interesting" shape is the result of not aligning squares of a pattern evenly.

16

Green and Pink Ladders

Two comments about Green and Pink Ladders: First, I love quilt artist Nancy Crow's work, which inspired this design. Second, it's easier to cut curves in woven fabric for a quilt than it is to knit curves, so the design presents challenges. The color palette (brown, pink, and several shades of green) for this rug is the same as that for Pink Swish (page 168) and was inspired by a couple of paint chips from the hardware store.

Looking at this rug critically, I see a few things I'd change were I to knit it again. I wish the rug had a center of interest, such as making one square considerably brighter than all the others, with several not-quite-as-bright squares surrounding it. Also, I had to cut up more strips of the light green when they ran out mid-rug. The added colors don't quite match, and that bothers me; the piece I tied in is a good bit brighter than the other greens. And finally, the actual rug is bigger than my original plan (4' × 6' instead of 3' × 5'), and I don't think this scaling up was an improvement. It would have been helpful to have drawn out the pattern at a much larger scale to see what was going to happen with the shapes.

Project Overview

- This rug consists of 15 vertical stripes, so it could just as easily be included in chapter 4, Earn Your Stripes. Because it involves some free-form knitting, it is included here instead.

- The asymmetrical color blocks that comprise each stripe are created by working short rows. The short rows lengthen the edge of the color blocks, so, in order to knit a flat piece, with relatively straight stripes, you must balance short rows worked on one edge of a stripe with short rows worked on the opposite edge. I have provided instructions for how to begin knitting one wide stripe and one narrow one. Use the same approach to work out the pattern for the other stripes.

KNITTING STRIPE #2

These row-by-row instructions show you how to begin the first wide stripe from the right (labeled #2 on the photo on the facing page). The concept is the same for each stripe, so make your own graph-paper plan, based on the photo, if you wish, or create your own design. Use short rows to distort the blocks, as shown in the directions for Stripe #2 that follow. Wherever possible, space short

row turns the entire height of the colored block, rather than bunching them up all in one place.

BLOCK #1: GREEN
Setup. Using green, cast on 11 stitches.

Next rows. Knit to end of each row until you have 4 garter-stitch ridges (two for each graph paper square).

BLOCK #2: BROWN
Next rows. Using brown, knit 2 garter-stitch ridges.

BLOCK #3: GREEN
The next block must be 4 garter-stitch ridges tall on the right-hand

side and 2 garter-stitch ridges tall on the left-hand side. This calls for short rows, which are most easily concealed when they are on the inside rows of a block of color, rather than knit along the rows where the color change happens. You can make the short rows any length you wish (nearly all the way across or just a few stitches), but stagger them from row to row. (For how to work short rows, see Wrap-and-Turn, page 139.)

Next rows. Using green, knit 1 garter-stitch ridge.

Short rows. Knit 2 garter-stitch ridges with short rows that start on the right-hand edge, taking care

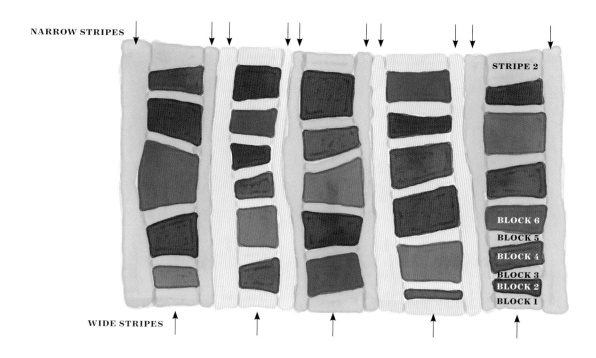

not to have them begin and end at the same distance from the edge.

Next rows. Knit 1 garter-stitch ridge.

BLOCK #4: OLIVE

Using olive, work 6 garter-stitch ridges, with no short rows.

BLOCK #5: GREEN

This is the reverse of Block #3, designed to bring the entire piece back into square, so it doesn't go too far off plumb. It must be 2 garter-stitch ridges tall on the right and 4 garter-stitch ridges

tall on the left. When this block is completed, you will have a distorted green block that angles the other direction from the first green block, and what you've knit so far should be roughly square.

Next rows. Knit 1 garter-stitch ridge.

Short row (wrong side). Knit 2 garter-stitch ridges with short rows starting on the left-hand edge any length you want, but staggered from one another.

Next rows. Knit 1 garter-stitch ridge.

BLOCKS #6 TO TOP

Continue to shape the remainder of the stripe in the same manner, alternating large and narrow blocks and using short rows to balance the overall garter-stitch ridge count. My rug has 56 garter-stitch ridges in each stripe. The wide stripes in the rest of the rug have 11 to 13 blocks, but you can vary those as well, as long as your overall ridge count for each stripe is the same.

NARROW STRIPES

Note that the total garter-stitch ridge count for this (and every) stripe must be 56. Instead of using short rows to create the undulations in the narrow stripes, each starts with a 7-stitch cast on, but then increases or decreases, as you can see in the photo. Make all increases and decreases on the same side of the stripe.

Setup. Using pale green, cast on 7 stitches, turn, and knit to end.

Knit even for 14 rows. (8 garter-stitch ridges of 7 stitches.)

Decrease. K2tog, knit to end on next right-side row, then knit even on wrong-side row. (6 stitches)

Work even for 14 more rows. (8 garter-stitch ridges of 6 stitches)

Decrease. K2tog, knit to end on next right-side row, then knit even on wrong-side row. (5 stitches)

Work even for 10 more rows. (6 garter-stitch ridges of 5 stitches)

Decrease. K2tog, knit to end on next right-side row, then knit even on wrong-side row. (4 stitches)

Work even for 6 more rows. (4 garter-stitch ridges of 4 stitches)

Decrease. K2tog, knit to end on next right-side row, then knit even on wrong-side row. (3 stitches)

Work even for 2 more rows. (2 garter-stitch ridges of 3 stitches)

Increase. Kfb, knit to end on next right-side row, then knit even on wrong-side row. (4 stitches)

Work even for 2 more rows. (2 garter-stitch ridges of 4 stitches)

Increase. Kfb, knit to end on next right-side row, then knit even on wrong-side row. (5 stitches)

Work even for 2 more rows. (2 garter-stitch ridges of 5 stitches)

Increase. Kfb, knit to end on next right-side row, then knit even on wrong-side row. (6 stitches)

Work even for 30 more rows. (16 garter-stitch ridges of 6 stitches)

Increase. Kfb, knit to end on next right-side row, then knit even on wrong-side row. (7 stitches)

Work even for 6 more rows. (8 garter-stitch ridges of 7 stitches) Bind off on the last wrong-side row.

Wondering whether a pattern inspired by a Nancy Crow quilt could be knit in garter-stitch stripes, I made my first design on plain white paper, rather than graph paper. After coloring in the squares and considering, I thought it was possible, so I sketched the design roughly on graph paper to help me keep track of how many stitches would be needed. The narrowest vertical stripe could be three stitches wide; the widest up to 12 or 13. To be easily seen, the horizontal dividing blocks had to be at least 2 garter-stitch ridges deep.

In the finished design, I distorted the blocks by knitting short rows, but in order to make a rug that lay flat, with strips all the same length, I had to first plan the total number of garter-stitch ridges needed top to bottom.

Two of the stripes (A stripes) have five dark blocks and three of the stripes (B stripes) have six dark blocks. The dark blocks in the A stripes have 8 garter-stitch ridges; the dark blocks in the B stripes have 7 garter-stitch ridges. Between the dark blocks in both A and B stripes are 2 light garter-stitch ridges.

At the top and bottom, the A stripes have 4 light garter-stitch ridges and the B stripes have 2 light garter-stitch ridges. The total garter-stitch ridge count for all stripes is 56. Figuring 2 ridges to the inch, this makes 27½ inches; the finished rug is 30 inches.

With this ridge count in mind, the next step in planning the design was to distort the blocks by curving them on the graph-paper sketch. I then laid out the number of stitches for each of the skinny stripes. For the wider stripes, I simply counted boxes on the graph paper, multiplied by 2 (stitches per inch), and planned to knit what was called for. When you're knitting this way, it's helpful to mark the transition points on the graph paper.

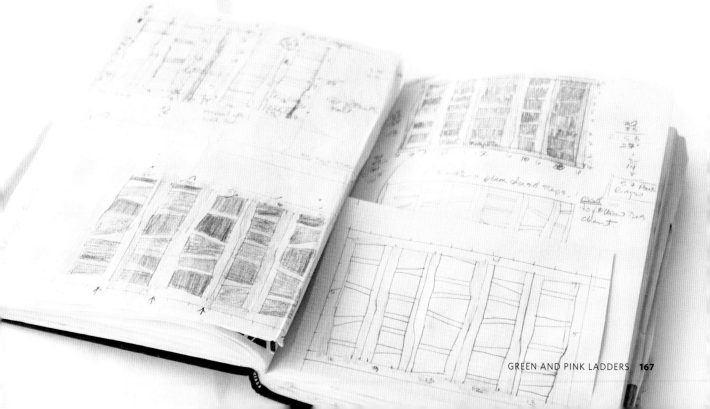

17 / Pink Swish

I sketched out the pattern for Pink Swish a dozen times in my notebook and played with shading and balance. Then I took a large canvas and painted the design to see what it would look like at the actual size of the rug. Next, I photographed my painted picture so I could mark the increases and short rows. (Paint was more cost effective and less time consuming than filling all those square inches with colored pencil.)

To make the pattern, I traced the shapes from the painting onto a big sheet of brown kraft paper, then cut the paper into pattern pieces. I knit the rug to fit the pattern pieces, laying the knitted piece over the paper to check every three or four rows.

The dark background corners are composed of simple stripes, but where they connect with the center "swish," the bottom (or top) of each one is shaped differently. I knit three stripes for the swishes: one of pink and two of pale green. To get the curves, I worked short rows, alternating long short rows and short short rows as needed. (See Wrap-and-Turn, page 139.) Where you have just a few garter-stitch ridges between short rows, use fewer stitches for the short rows; where you need a gentle curve, knit more stitches before you turn. Be sure to stagger the short rows.

18 / Purple and Orange Climbing Bars

urple and Orange Climbing Bars is an extreme application of the Floating Gold Square pattern, (page 76). At times it appeared to be almost unknittable. It was finally finished as I sat on the floor, knitting row by row and checking the piece on the needles against the rest of the completed, assembled rug, just two days before the scheduled photo shoot for this book. That said, now that it's done and the pain and frustration has faded, it is a fine rug. Here are the general instructions, and some notes about where I got into trouble.

The purple-to-lavender background is composed of three wide stripes, each of which is made up of three narrower stripes, just like those in Floating Square. I wrote out a plan for transitioning eight shades of purple for these stripes. That was the easy part. Figuring out the placement and transition of the floating orange bars was something else again, as it meant designing several color strips that were half orange and half purple

in the same row/ridge. For example, the first two orange bars at the bottom of the rug end halfway through vertical stripe #5; bar C starts halfway through stripe #2; and so forth. The bars shift to the right by a number of stitches that looked good on graph paper, but it was very difficult to keep track of right and wrong sides, top and bottom of the pattern, when to cast off (and on which side) to leave room for insets, when to change from orange to purple, and so on.

One approach I took to working these two-color stripes was to bind off one of the colors, knit up with the other for just the width of the bar, then cast on again, leaving a space into which I could insert a new piece knit in the other color to complete the bar. Note that the orange also shades from dark at the bottom to light at the top.

If you'd like to try to knit this rug, have fun. But don't say I didn't warn you!

itch Counts for ertical Stripes

PE	NUMBER OF STITCHES
Left 1	6
Left 2	8
Left 3	6
Center 1	7
Center 2	8
Center 3	7
Right 1	6
Right 2	8
Right 3	6

Color Progression

A is the lightest shade.

COLOR	NUMBER OF GARTER-STITCH RIDGES	COLOR	NUMBER OF GARTER-STITCH RIDGES
A	7	E	1
B	1	D	1
A	1	E	1
B	1	D	1
A	1	E	13
B	3	F	1
C	1	E	1
B	1	F	1
C	1	E	1
B	1	F	14
C	3	G	1
D	1	F	1
C	1	G	1
D	1	F	1
C	1	G	12
D	13		

Metric Conversion Chart

TO CONVERT	TO	MULTIPLY
inches	millimeters	inches by 25.4
inches	centimeters	inches by 2.54

How to Read the Charts

Read all charts starting at the bottom right. When you complete row 1, read the next row up (row 2) from left to right. For motif like triangles and diamonds, notice that all increases (and decreases) are made at the beginning of rows, as indicated by one more (or one fewer) square at that point. Each square equals 1 row and 1 stitch.

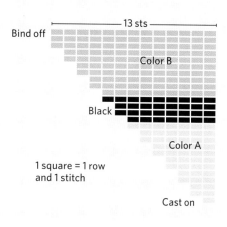

Bind off

13 sts

Color B

Black

Color A

1 square = 1 row
and 1 stitch

Cast on

Index

Acknowledgments

I would like to thank:

Gwen Steege, Alethea Morrison, and all the staff at Storey who made this book so much more than it was in the proposal.

Kip Dawkins and Marcie Blough for the images, and also their associates for the location and styling.

Every author of every book about knitting that expanded my thinking in different directions; I'm afraid to name any for fear of leaving someone out. In addition to those already mentioned in the book, Sabrina Gschwandtner, Debbie New, Mary Walker Phillips, Barbara Walker, and Maggie Righetti (who probably doesn't remember being interviewed by me for a review), and most of all, of course, Elizabeth Zimmermann.

And finally, the weavers and volunteers working for the Outer Banks Hotline and Endless Possibilities Gallery, where I first saw used clothing being cut up for fiber.